Up River

Wayne Coggins

To Paul + Janice,
Enjoy this walk back in time.
Lots of good memories with you –
Wayne + his earthly partner
Maureen

Raven Publishing, Inc.
Norris, MT

Up River

ISBN: 978-1-937849-87-0
Cover photo: Skagit River and Eldorado Peak, © Ron Clausen
Creative Commons Attribution-Share Alike 4.0 International
Raven Publishing, Inc.
PO Box 2866, Norris, MT 59745
www.ravenpublishing.net

Printed in the United States

Library of Congress Cataloging in Publication Data (pending)

LCCN: 2021014471

To the memory of my parents,

Glenn and Eileen Coggins

Thank you!

Contents

Prologue
It's Been a Good Life All in All

One of my prized possessions is a three CD collection of the greatest hits of John Denver. He was and still is one of my favorite song-writers and singers. Among a whole bunch of "favorite" songs is "Poems, Prayers, and Promises". (John Denver, RCA Victor, 1971) While a few of the lyrics are not reflective of my values or my way of speaking, several phrases always capture my thoughts and send me sailing into some serious scans of my memory.

The song opens with, "I've been lately thinking about my lifetime, about all the things I've done and how it's been..." At age 74, I tend to often reflect back on my life and "how it's been." More than once I have found my eyes brimming with tears of gratitude as my mind frames pictures of people I have known and loved, as well as some of the wonderful experiences and adventures that I've had.

Later in the song's refrain, Denver sings, "I have to say it now it's been a good life all in all. It's really nice to have a chance to hang around..." I imagine that track is about worn out as I hit the replay button to hear it again and again.

Yes, it has been a good life all in all! I have been a blessed man. Like most people experience, there have been those seasons in my life where I had to drink deep from the well of God's mercy, grace, and forgiveness to get through some rough waters. But I have to say that God's love and that of my family and friends has been faithful, steady, and sure.

Up River

I have saved an old letter written to my mother by her life-long friend and mentor, Ruby Krook, when I was in high school. In it, she said, "I have been praying for Wayne that the Lord will keep the sideboards up on that boy. He seems a little wobbly lately." With allies like that, I feel like a very rich person in the things that really matter.

Chapter 1

To Set the Stage... Lyman 1956

It was 1956 and I was ten years old, growing up in the little town of Lyman, Washington, an old logging town in the Pacific Northwest and on the Skagit River with a pretty steady population of about 400 people. World War II had ended on September 12, 1945 and the boys, including my dad, came home to rebuild their lives and families. 1946 is the official start of the "baby boom" of which I am happy to be a part. There were 75.8 million babies born in America during that period (1946-1964) and in my birth year, there were 3,410,000 of us that made our appearance.

Growing up during the 40's, 50's and into the 60's was a great time from my perspective. It has often been described as a "simpler time" when it seemed like life's pace was much slower and more anchored in traditional American values. We sang Christmas songs in school, gave each other Valentine's Day cards, and got spanked at both school and home if we got caught doing forbidden stuff.

In 1956, I lived to play little league baseball on the Lyman -Hamilton Loggers team. Ed Fore was the coach and, looking back, I think he was the best coach I ever had. That was the year the World Series was a New York affair with the NY Yankees beating the Brooklyn Dodgers in seven games. Yogi Berra and Mickey Mantle were household names and were my heroes. When I wasn't playing or practicing baseball, along with the rest of Lyman's ten-year-olds, I picked strawberries to earn money for school clothes for the next year. Later in the fall I'd pick blackberries and sell them to the cannery buyer for five cents a pound and usually make enough to buy a bag of peanuts and an RC Cola which were combined to make a great reward.

Lyman had four main areas. They were the west side where we lived, the mid-town area where the City Park and Cemetery were, the main part of the town south of the railroad tracks known as "Uptown" and the east side where there was an old CCC (Civilian Conservation Corps) Camp. The Uptown of Lyman had the Post Office, Koop's Lyman Market, the Lyman Tavern, the City Hall and jail, and the little church we attended, all of which were so close I could stand in one place and hit each with a rock.

Also, within rock-range was the Jackpot Café next to the railroad tracks. It was a huge treat when we had a dollar or two to spend and could afford to have a "store bought" hamburger, some chips and a fountain Coke. It had a U-shaped counter on which were some of those little tune selectors where you could drop a quarter in the slot and select three or four country or early rock and roll hits that played in the big juke box over next to the pinball machine. On the juke box was Elvis belting out "Heartbreak Hotel" or crooning "Love Me Tender", both of which were pretty much lost on me since, at ten years-old, I wasn't much into that mushy-lovey-dovey stuff as I was into baseball, fishing for trout in the river or local creeks, or wandering the hills looking for adventure.

Black and white television was relatively new, so you could often find us kids glued to the TV, sure not to miss the Mickey Mouse Club, Ozzie and Harriet, or Gunsmoke. However, in 1956, radio dramas were still popular and Saturday afternoons would find me sitting in front of our big console radio listening with baited breath to the adventures of The Lone Ranger and Tonto. Once a year they would broadcast an elongated version of how the Lone Ranger came to wear his trademark mask and how he and Tonto had become sidekicks and allies in their quest to bring the bad guys to justice in the old west.

I grew up a middle child with a sister four years older than me and one four years younger. Later, when I was twelve, my long-desired brother joined the scene. When our dad, came home from World War II, he got a job as an occupational therapist at Northern State (mental) Hospital where he worked in conjunction with the psychiatrists, finding meaningful tasks for the residents to aid in their recovery. Everyday he'd drive his old Model A Ford the nine miles from our house to the hospital. He was an LPN and, before work he would make the early morning rounds in the area to help several old-timers with their insulin shots, then pick up a coworker and head for the hospital. He was a city councilman and once, during an illness of the mayor, he served as "mayor pro-tem" of our little town. I don't remember him ever putting up a campaign sign or giving a campaign speech, rather; they just always put his name, Glenn R. Coggins, on the ballot and he got re-elected.

My mom was a stay-at-home mom while I was growing up, but later, she worked at the elementary school as the attendance secretary. She also was the town clerk for a while and worked every election on the election board. Beside those civic activities, she was our church pianist, was Sunday school superintendent, where she taught the adult class, and was a deaconess in the church. She was also "in demand" by one of the local Gospel "tarheel" quartets who would call the house asking, "Can Eileen come and help us make music?" She fully espoused the philosophy that the best way to keep her kids out of trouble was to keep them in church and busy with sports and other activities.

So, that overview I have tried to describe is the background for the experiences that are coming in the pages ahead. I will have changed the names of some of the characters if their role in the story would be embarrassing for them, their children, or grandchildren. My hope is that these stories will give the reader some idea of life in Lyman back then. It is not a history of the town but just my memories of how it was for me.

Guilty as Charged

If being nostalgic were a crime, I would have to admit being guilty as charged. The Oxford Dictionary defines it this way: "Nostalgia: A sentimental longing or wistful affection for the past, typically for a period or place with happy personal associations."

Chapter 2

Entering Lyman

ENTERING LYMAN, WA
POPULATION 400
DRIVE SLOWLY

That was the sign that stood next to our mailbox on the west end of this quiet little town in rural Washington State. We lived at the edge of the city limits just off the "old road" that ran through the town. Also next to our mailbox was the infamous 25 mph speed limit sign that was strictly enforced by Curly, the town policeman. For years that was the only road on the north side of the Skagit River, leading east up the valley until the state constructed the new Highway 20 that bypassed the town.

It was like growing up in Mayberry, USA where Andy Griffith, Opie, Aunt Bea and Barney Fife became TV household names. Old rural values and traditions reigned. It had the most incredible creek-fed water supply before chlorination became a requirement, never mind that the pipeline that brought that sweet water down the mountain ran right through the base of the ravine that was the town garbage dump!

Lyman had some definitely colorful characters with equally colorful names or nicknames. I remember hearing names like Stoggie Parker, Yuler Aiken, Fat Cabe, Stob Self, and of course my grandpa, Make, whose real name was Malcolm, but I didn't know that until they put it on his tombstone. I was in high school when he died.

Other than the "plunkin' shack fishing hole" on the south side of town, there were two special places in Lyman. One was a specific place and the other was a general location. Like a lot of small old towns in America, there was a gathering place (not including the tavern) where old timers would sit and talk, share stories, lies, and whatever might be the hot topic in town, like how outrageous it was that the cost of the monthly water bill was going up from $3.00 a month to $5.00. It was the barber shop. I remember going there to get my hair cut, and while waiting my turn, would hear the old timers philosophizing or holding forth on some issue or matter of personal conviction. In a small way, it was one of the places where the town's values, legends and traditions were passed down from one generation to the next. Some of what was discussed was good stuff you would want to put in the foundation of your life. Some of it was…baloney!

The other place where such discussions were held was on the big front porches that were common to most of the houses in Lyman. These were not the "fortress" houses that became popular when subdivisions and tract houses were invented. They were old frame houses that were so narrow you could often see straight through them from the front door to the back. In the evenings, families would gather on those old porches, drink iced tea (or sometimes beer) and moms, dads, kids, and grandparents would talk about life and the things that mattered to those gathered. Questions were asked, dilemmas discussed, suggestions given, life lessons passed on and values imparted. This was not the scene at every house to be sure, but it was still pretty common.

In the Bible, there were the gates of the city where (along with the beggars) the elders of the city would gather to share stories, resolve disputes, and share their wisdom and hard-earned lessons of life. It was considered a position of honor and respect to be able to "sit at the gates."

Other places in our town where good things were passed on were the family dinner tables, the local school, and of course the local churches. I will talk about those later. And, lest the reader might think that my memories of growing up in the fifties and sixties in this little town sound way too idyllic to be true, like any town in the USA, there were occasionally great tragedies and the town had a policeman and a small jail for a reason. However, these are my memories and I think the good stuff far outweighed the bad.

CHAPTER 3

Sunrise — Sunset

WATCHING LYMAN WAKE UP

Our little town, situated in the Skagit River Valley, was surrounded by mountains. The Skagit River ran east to west, giving us vistas of incredible sunrises and sunsets in those directions. Growing up, the sunrises and sunsets were often too spectacular for my little Brownie Instamatic Camera to capture a picture that did them justice.

I'm sure I enjoyed more sunsets than sunrises since most evenings were spent either doing farm chores or playing outside until dark. However, there were a couple of years when I had a morning paper route that allowed me to enjoy the early morning sunrises as I rode my bike all over town making my deliveries. It gave me a whole new appreciation for the silence and solitude that occurred as the little town was awakening. The smell of wood smoke and frying bacon filled the air. The dew was heavy on the grass and the dandelions would have their heads bowed, waiting for the morning sun to spray its warmth on them as their wake-up call to rise and shine. The job didn't pay much, but I did enjoy the early morning race against the clock to see if I could beat my record in completing my route. It usually took about an hour.

The two things I did not enjoy were collection day and delivering papers to houses with loose dogs that seemed to revel in chasing the paper boy. Only a couple of times did one big German Shepherd manage to get a bite of my blue jeans as I would be at full speed ahead in enemy territory. I had a squirt gun taped to the handle bars of my bike loaded with some diluted ammonia as ammo, but I usually missed my target. The obnoxious smell, however, caused the dog to call off the chase.

Being painfully shy made collection day the last Saturday of the month a big challenge for me. Knocking on the doors was an ordeal. I almost always had the papers delivered on time and in the desired location, so I'd often get a dollar or two as a tip, or sometimes a baggie of cookies.

We didn't get much snow in the winter but when we did, my mom was always willing to crawl out of bed and drive me around to make the deliveries. If I were sick, she would do the whole route for me.

Looking back, I am grateful for the lessons in responsibility that job taught me. To this day, I still love to watch the early morning sunrise. Near the finale of the movie, "Quigley Down Under," the actor, Tom Selleck, tells his sweetheart, "You shor' look pretty in the mornin' sun." So did Lyman.

Chapter 4

Up River

From my second floor, south facing, bedroom window, I could see a stretch of the Skagit River as it flowed from left to right. It was pretty common for my dad to call up through the heat vent early in the morning for me to give him a report on the river conditions. Too high? Too muddy? Or, "Looks good from here." Sometimes my report would weigh heavily on whether or not Dad would go fishing.

Sometimes, if there had been days of monsoon rains or warm chinook winds that would have the river running way too high and muddy for fishing, that would be a signal for my dad to take a long pole with a little net on the end and pay a visit to several log jams or eddies. There, he would find numerous floating "wing bobbers" or other fishing lures floating in the sticks, bark, or other trash that gathered there. He rarely had to buy any of those floating lures, but kept his growing stash in the garage as his own sporting goods supply store.

In fact, when Dad passed away at 79 years of age, he had six

3-pound coffee cans full of those reclaimed lures. My brother and I divvied them up, three cans each. We used quite a few of the good ones for fishing, but in order to preserve the memory, I strung a bunch of them into necklaces, one of which my wife still tenaciously guards lest I rob the colorful string of a few of the "special" ones.

The Skagit River could be dangerous to careless fishermen, and in the 50's there were scores of guides and locals who plied its waters as a prime fishery for steelhead and salmon. Occasionally, due to motor failure or boat driver carelessness, a boat would drift sideways into a log jam causing it to capsize, and sometimes lives were lost. Sometimes the eddies would have more than fishing lures floating in them!

Knowing the potential dangers that lurked across the field and railroad tracks at THE RIVER, I regularly received sobering exhortations to be careful if I were heading over there to go fishing myself. "Watch out for slick rocks or the places where the banks are being eroded by the strong currents." It was fairly common to hear a loud "splash" as 5 or 6 feet of former pastureland would suddenly plunge into the water. I would acknowledge their warnings were wise and be grateful I had heeded them and was not standing on that eroding spot.

For all of its dangers and conditions, the river was a source of great joy for me where I spent countless hours fishing, exploring, or sitting on a rock or log, daydreaming about what I would do when I grew up. I had great fun when I found a stretch of shoreline comprised of perfectly rounded and flat rocks that were ideal for skipping across the water. I think my personal best was 23 skips before the rock finally sank. There were also several stretches of shore where the rocks were predominately round, golf-ball size, tailor made for throwing at a stick floating downstream or, for finding a piece of dried driftwood about the size of a baseball bat and tossing a stone in the air and smacking it, sometimes, clear across the river.

Later when I began to attend high school in the town of Sedro Woolley, about 9 miles downstream, I remember our school song started out with the words, "Here beside the Skagit River, stands our school so bold..." Actually, I thought the best fun was to be found 9 miles back "upriver" where I grew up. Today, I cherish those river memories, and sort of feel sorry for children who grow up in cities. You can't find such adventures at the mall.

Chapter 5

Our Sow Susie

Now, before I pass on this story from my life on the farm, let me please make an apology to any lady whose name is Suzy or Susie, by saying that we named our Hampshire brood sow, Susie, not after any of them. Please do not be offended. In fact, we had two neighbor girls with that name and both bore no resemblance to "our" Susie. In reality, I remember them both being as cute as could be. The name came from the old farm practice of hog-calling that went something like "Soooooeeee, soooooeeee! Pig, Pig, Pig, Pig." In our case, we just added, "Come on Susie," and would rap an old stirring spoon on the side of her slop bucket at feeding time and Susie would come running.

During my grade school years, I was more than a little acquainted with Susie because a part of my after school/evening chores was often to mix up some mash with some scraps of food (appropriately called "pig slop") and trudge out back to the pig pen and pour it into a feed trough for her evening of fine dining. There is more to that story, but that is another chapter called "Piggins and Porkchop".

Susie was actually a pretty friendly old gal and absolutely loved it when I'd use a garden hoe to scratch her back now and then. She'd just stand there with what looked to me like a very contented look on her snout, occasionally "oink," usually lie down on her side in the dirt or mud, close her eyes, and take an after-dinner nap.

Once in a while, Susie would find a way to escape her pen and would head out across our neighbor's pasture to see what adventures might await there. Either we'd notice that she was gone or one of the neighbors would call us on the old party line, VA-236 number, and say, " Ol' Susie is out in Ally's pasture again." Thankfully, Ally had a good fence between his pasture and Highway 20 so she wasn't able to get out on the road and be turned into sausage by one of the many logging trucks that often came roaring by.

Now, I suppose it is technically possible to lasso a 400-pound pig around the neck and hop on and ride her back to the gap in the fence where she'd escaped, but believe me, she'd have none of that. Trying to cajole or drive a stubborn freedom-loving pig presents yet a whole different set of challenges, perhaps akin to that old adage that, "You can't teach a pig to sing. Frustrates you and irritates the pig." It wasn't rocket science to figure out how to get her to come running if we'd stand in her pen by the escape hole, bang on that old "slop bucket" and holler loudly "Sooooeee! Pig, Pig, Pig! Come on, Susie," and here she'd come running as fast as her short pig legs could carry her fat body.

Probably the most fun part of caring for Susie was when she'd be giving birth to a litter of piglets, usually 12-14 of the cutest little squeakers. A few times I was able to be present to observe the whole process. Susie would be lying on her side when she'd grunt and "blurp." Out would pop a little baby pig, struggling to get out of its opaque birth sac. Sometimes Susie would have to help them along. Then, instinct would kick in, and a frenzy of activity would ensue, as all of those little tykes would climb over each other, trying to locate an available faucet for their first meal.

Over the years, Susie had sustained a few injuries so not all of her faucets were fully operational. Sometimes there weren't enough functional ones to go around. One year, with a dozen or so little piglets all lined up being fed, we noticed one timid little runt that wasn't big or strong enough to muscle his way into the line-up at a working unit. Figuring he would not survive, we took the little guy into the house, put him in a cardboard box by the old wood stove in the utility room, and proceeded to bottle-feed him. A few days later when a couple of his birth buddies died for some reason, we were able to put him back into the general population.

By that time my sisters and I had pretty much bonded with the cute little guy, and despite knowing that it was not wise to give farm animals destined for someone's dinner table a name, we gave him one. At the time there was a heavyweight boxer that was going to fight the champion and was considered a huge underdog. The boxer's name was Pete Rademaker…so we named our "under-pig" Rademaker. It was a sad day, a few weeks later, when Rademaker was sold, put into the back of someone's pick-up, and hauled off to his destiny.

After the young pigs were big and old enough to be weaned from Susie, the word would go out and the buyers would come to pick up their critter. The usual plan was for us to corner and catch their choice, put it wiggling and squirming into a burlap feed sack, and then tie it shut to prevent escape. Well, one day as we were loading an energetic little guy into the trunk of someone's car, he managed to wiggle so much the knot on the sack came loose and he escaped into the yard and then into an adjacent muddy corn field. Now, catching a loosed greased little piggy is indeed a fun sport at the rodeo, but this little fellow was faster than your average pig. Three or four of us managed to corner him by the fence and when he made a break for it, my mom, dressed in her blue jeans and muck boots, made a dive for him and managed to grab him by one hind leg. Mom was as determined to hang on as the pig was to escape. The pig, with four-wheel (leg) drive was digging with both front legs and one hind leg, which, in that muddy field, meant that it was kicking a barrage of clumps of soggy wet mud onto Mom's face, hair, and glasses. The rest of us were paralyzed with laughter at Mom and that squealing wide- eyed little pig until Mom yelled for one of us to bring that blasted gunny sack and get that thing back into it and into the buyer's trunk.

Whoever thinks there is never any fun and adventure on a farm should have been there that day. For years that story was told and re-told whenever the family would gather for holiday story-fests.

Chapter 6

Buying Gifts

A few years ago, a book entitled *The Five Love Languages* by Gary Chapman (Northfield Publishing, Chicago, IL, 1992) came out. It is a fascinating explanation of the five basic love languages, or the ways we tend to best give or receive love. They were physical touch, practical service, words of endearment, quality time, and giving of gifts. Personally, I like all five, but after some evaluation of the storyline of my life, I learned that there was one area that was going to need some work.

An experience that I had as a boy of 9 or 10 pointed to the fact that I was somewhat deficient in the area of giving of gifts. Mother's Day was approaching and I was drawing a blank as to what to get my mom as a gift. I had a few dollars saved up but I couldn't think of a thing my mom might need or want. So, in desperation, I asked my dad if he had any ideas. He was probably the last person to ask as Dad was probably one of the most practical men on the planet. His reply was, "Just get her something practical."

Armed with that bit of sage advice, the next Saturday when Mom had some shopping to do in Sedro Woolley, I asked to be dropped off at the Coast to Coast hardware store, one of my favorite stores, because they also sold fishing tackle and BB guns along with "practical" stuff galore. In I went like a man on a mission to bag a gift for Mom. Up and down the long aisles of the store I went, scanning from side to side for something in the ten-dollar range.

We had plenty of hammers, screw drivers, paint, and staples. I was about to ask a clerk for some suggestions when I saw it. Ah-ha! Indeed, it was a practical gift for my mom that I was sure she'd really love and appreciate. I knew we already had one but it was pretty worn and ugly. This one was new and shiny and really quite nice for only $7.95 plus tax.

The clerk had a strange expression when I asked if he could gift wrap it for me, but I had the look of a victorious big game hunter so he went along with me and put some pretty paper around it. I walked out of that store with a swagger like I had just bagged a trophy deer.

The next day was Mother's Day and, after church and dinner, we all sat around the table before dessert, and Mom began to open her cards and gifts from her family. I was on the edge of my seat when she finally came to mine as I was sure she'd be overwhelmed with gratitude for my lovingly selected gift. She acknowledged that it was kind of heavy as she peeled the tape off the paper and folded it back to reveal the gift. It was silent around the table when the gift was revealed. It was a nice shiny set of...BATHROOM SCALES! I had gotten my mom a set of bathroom scales for Mother's Day. My dad looked sheepish, my sisters looked aghast, and my mom started crying, not tears of joy, but tears of disappointment. I was confused and crestfallen. It turns out that Mom was in one of her chubbier phases and mistook my intention as being a hint that she was too fat.

As soon as I got the chance, I cornered my dad who agreed to take me back to town where we could exchange the gift for one perhaps more suitable. A few days later Dad and I went back to the Coast to Coast store, and I exchanged the scales for a nice little bottle of lilac smelling perfume. When we got home, I presented it to Mom and felt her love and forgiveness as she said she loved that (sickeningly sweet) fragrance.

The bottom line here is found in the Bible verse which says there is safety in a multitude of counselors. So now, in my more mature years, I ask around before I give my wife yet another fishing pole or reel that I am sure will make her swoon with happiness.

CHAPTER 7

Ilo Sandy

In the '50s and '60s it was not unusual to have traveling salesmen knock on our door. If my mom was the one who answered the door, she'd feel sorry for the person and spend a few dollars. For several years running, a poor old fellow with St. Vitus Dance (the shakes) would come calling, selling greeting cards, and Mom usually bought one of everything he had.

The apple tree salesman was not so fortunate as he showed up on a Saturday afternoon when my dad was home and eating lunch. My dad was not rude, but neither was he a soft touch. After an hour or two of wrangling, the salesman called his home office and got the green light to plant about ten dwarf transparent apple trees along one of our fences as a demo-project for free.

I remember one life insurance salesman named Ilo Sandy (a name easy to remember). He visited our house several evenings in an attempt to convince my dad to sign on the dotted line for some insurance. I remember that he wore leg braces and walked with some difficulty, using some short crutches. He shared that he'd been a victim of polio years before. He was a determined salesman but my dad was not an easy sell.

Well, one night as he was doing his best to convince my dad to buy his company's program, my dad stepped out of the room for some reason and Mr. Sandy spied me sitting on the couch tossing a baseball into my baseball mitt. I was probably 11 years old and loved baseball. He called me over by his chair and asked me what position I played, to which I replied, "third base or pitcher." "Here," he said, "let me show you a secret weapon," which was how to hold and throw a knuckleball. He had played baseball before being stricken with polio, and I was all eyes and ears. I had heard about a knuckleball, watching television or listening to the Seattle Rainiers games on the radio, but had no clue how to throw one. He showed me how to grip the ball and make it spring off my fingertips so the ball had little or no spin enroute to home plate. The ball would jump or dive unpredictably and was very hard to catch and equally hard for the batter to hit.

I practiced and practiced that pitch for years, but it wasn't until my junior year in high school that I could finally get it in the strike zone about half the time. It was hilarious to watch the hitters swing and miss by a mile. That was the year that we had a rain-shortened seven-inning non-league game against a small school in the area. Because the ball was usually wet, it was to the pitcher's advantage for throwing curves or even a knuckleball. It was the top of the 7th inning when I discovered that I had a no hitter going. Gulp! The first two batters were relatively easy to get out, but the other coach decided to give the last player on the bench a chance to pinch hit. He was a pretty chunky guy and I was fairly certain he would be easy to strike out. I threw him a knuckleball and, to everyone's surprise, that guy closed his eyes and hit a hard line drive to right field. The right fielder was playing in close and fielded the ball on one hop and, since the hitter was pretty slow afoot, actually threw him out before he got to first base, and saved my one and only no-hitter!

I don't think my dad ever bought life insurance from Ilo Sandy, but this young boy never forgot him. I thought of him often as I tried to master the gift he'd given me.

Chapter 8

The Most Unlikely Treasurer

The pattern began to emerge pretty early in my life that a math whiz I was not. Mr. Roe, the stern 6th grade teacher and principal at Lyman Grade School, wrote a note on my report card that said, "Wayne does pretty well in language arts and spelling, but he can't seem to bother with decimal points." Math was not my forte. I could tell you the batting averages of the New York Yankees, but if asked to multiply fractions, my brain went out to recess.

I never could figure out algebra in 9th grade, but a cute little blonde named Sandy tutored me enough that I managed to squeak by. It was a mystery to me how numbers and letters had any business trying to logically connect. Sometimes I think Mr. Harris, the algebra teacher, who was also the baseball coach, just had mercy on me because I was a pretty decent third baseman.

Then came high school, and with it, I had dreams of playing baseball in college and somehow getting drafted to play for the Yankees. The problem did not lie in whether I had the drive to reach toward that goal, but I would have to climb Mt. Geometry to get there. I was lost in that class right after Mr. Jones called the roll on that first day. However, I knew there was a God in heaven when my assigned seat was right in front of a cute redhead, Megan, who was the teacher's daughter. I figured she ate geometric Cheerios for breakfast. She was always on the honor roll, and my good fortune was that she had mercy on me, and many times would take the time to try to help me understand how this theorem or that rule in math applied to a problem. That I never really "got" algebra didn't help much. But, with Megan's help, I passed geometry and kept my grade point average up high enough so I didn't get disqualified from playing on the baseball team.

Toward the end of my junior year, when elections were held for student body and class officers for the next year, I don't know who did it, but somebody nominated me to be the Associated Student Body Treasurer. I remember thinking, why on earth would anyone think for a minute that I could look at rows of numbers and figure out how to report to the Student Council which club or fund had how much money to work with.

To top it off, I was running against a really good looking and smart guy who was a varsity football star. Then, each candidate had to stand up in front of the whole school and give a speech about why he or she would be a good officer. I tried to figure out a way to weasel out of that terrifying experience, but after a week of sleepless nights, my name was called, and out on the stage I clomped with a fist full of note cards. Somehow, I squeaked through that gauntlet and the next day found out that I had won and would get my picture in the yearbook as an ASB officer.

The next school year began and an "angel" appeared in the form of May Kirkpatrick who worked in the school office and happened to be one of my mother's best friends and a close neighbor. May had mercy on me and every month she'd hand me a balance sheet of the financial state of the school organizations.

All I had to do was read the bottom line in each column. Shoot, that was easier by far than trying to hit a 90-mph fastball or turn a double play.

I did eventually learn to balance a check book and figure out how to do decimal points to figure out a 10% discount on fishing gear.

Chapter 9

The Sure Cure

Back in the fifties there wasn't much of a push that connected smoking with cancer, so it seemed like a lot of people in our town smoked cigarettes, cigars, chewed tobacco, or had a lower lip full of "snoose," as it was called back then. My dad smoked a pipe, and it seemed like no big deal. However, at the little church we attended, smoking was often preached about as one of the "big bad sins" and was definitely a highly discouraged activity.

Like most young boys, hearing about anything that is forbidden sparked a growing curiosity to give it a try just once to see what it was like. One day a neighbor buddy and I were out walking along the road between my house and his and noticed there were a lot of old partially smoked cigarettes lying in the gravel shoulder of the road. I'm not sure whose lame idea it was, but we picked up a couple of handfuls of them, stopped by his house for a box of matches, and hid out behind their barn to light them up. We hacked and coughed and spit like crazy but managed to smoke several of those nasty tasting things before we started feeling kind of crummy, and abandoned our "sinful" experiment. Personally, that was enough for me and I was never tempted to smoke after that.

Another thing that kept me on the straight and narrow path in high school was baseball. I had a great love of baseball, and one of the school rules that was enforced was if you got caught smoking (or drinking) you would get kicked off the team. That potential fate made it easy for me to say no when offered a cigarette by some of my friends.

There was, however, no seeming prohibition on using "chaw", a stringy loose form of tobacco which, during that era, was commonly used by some of my major league heroes. One day someone brought a pouch of that stuff to baseball practice and, along with several others, I stuffed a wad of it in my mouth just as the coach started hitting grounders to us for infield practice. I was playing third base at the time. It didn't take long to realize that "chaw" tasted awful and it felt like it was burning a hole in my cheek. I was just about to spit the whole thing out when the coach hit a hard ground ball my way. Our field wasn't the smoothest field around and the ball hit a loose pebble and took an unexpected high hop right in front of me and bounced up and hit me hard right on my diaphragm which caused a reflex action on my part, and I accidentally swallowed the whole wad of that slimy tobacco. It wasn't long before I was off in the high grass beside the ball field upchucking the offending "chaw". NEVER AGAIN.

I am thankful for all of those youthful motivations to stay away from the habit of smoking. Like a number of negative or harmful habits, they are a lot easier to develop than they are to stop later on in life.

Chapter 10

Earthy

For the past 50-plus years, I have been blessed to serve the Lord and His people as a pastor and/or counselor. During those years, various folks have tried to describe my preaching. I can't remember it ever being described as "eloquent" or "polished." Probably the most common attempt has been either "down to earth" or just plain "earthy." Perhaps the following vignettes from my formative years will help clarify in part why the term "earthy" might just be my style.

Being raised on a small farm in an area of many larger dairy farms, I have many memories of some of the less than idyllic aspects of farm life. Be it mucking out the barnyard or the chicken coup, I think if there were a diploma in "shovel-hood," I probably earned one.

During my high school years, the spring and summer haying season was the mainstay of how boys like me made our school clothes money and kept our gas tanks full for the Friday and Saturday night ritual of driving back and forth on the main street in the nearby town of Sedro Woolley. Thanks to some patient tutoring I got in operating farm equipment, I was able to get a plum job working for a few local farmers. Once their fields were taken care of, they would hire me and their equipment out to other farmers who had fields of hay to get in but didn't have all the right equipment. I would cut and rake the grass into windrows and then bale the hay in to stackable bales. If I didn't have another job to go to, I'd often join the crew walking along beside a big flatbed truck, tossing the bales up so another guy could stack them, usually 5-6 bales high, for the trip to the barn where another crew would stack them for winter feed for the farmer's herd of cows.

In western Washington, we would have a week or so of sunshine, so the haying process would produce a barn full of sun and wind-dried hay. However, there were also many times when the job would be interrupted by a rain shower or sometimes a days-long deluge complicating the whole process. One day a crew of us guys were told that a bad rainstorm was on the way and we still had about 40-acres of baled hay on the ground. We were told that we'd likely need to work late into the night to get it all in the barn before the rain started to fall.

After working all day in the humid heat, it was closing in on midnight when finally, weary and sweaty, we just had a few bales around the perimeter to bring in. The truck driver let me off near a couple of stray bales and then continued on to the far end of the field to get a few more stray bales, planning then to head back for me and my batch. Having about a five-minute wait, I lay down in the cool grass to wait while the first drops of rain started to fall. Ahhhh. That cool, slightly damp grass felt great. Soon the truck pulled up, I tossed my load up and climbed aboard for the trip to the barn. As we neared the flood lights on the barn, my partner asked me what in the world was on the back of my shirt? Thinking it was just wet from my rest on the ground, I didn't think it was anything but damp. That is until we got to the barn and I realized that a few cows had been let into that newly mown field and what I had done was to lie down in a freshly deposited "cow pie!" Eeeuuuwww!

Before heading for home, I hosed off my shirt. One thing I knew for sure; my mom would not have been a happy mama to find that slimy mess in her laundry hamper. Is there a moral to this story? You bet'cha. Don't ever lie down on the job.

Who Flung Dung!

That expression went along with an old joke from school days. Perhaps the details would best be omitted here, but let me share a story of what farm kids might do for fun on occasion.

My friend, Curtis, and I were walking through the pasture behind their barn toward the river to pick blackberries when we noticed that there was an abundance of old dried out "cow pies" in the grass. So, being boys, we picked some up and flung them like frizbees. Soon we were chucking them at each other. They usually disintegrated before they hit you so it was just a fun, friendly war. After a while, I was running low on ammo when I noticed a fresh cow pie in the weeds, so I picked up a piece of broken roof shingle, scooped up a blob, and flung it at Curtis. He ducked too late, and it splatted on the side of his face! Oops. Our friendly war suddenly turned serious and Curtis came after me with revenge written all over his face. Now, I never was very fleet afoot, but I was highly motivated and outran him the mile or so to our house where he gave up the chase. Not much of a moral to this story, either, except to be grateful if you have friends that are quick forgivers.

There is one more "earthy" story I will share before moving on to more edifying subjects. Just out of high school, one of my first jobs was working for the Skagit-Island County Dairy Herd Improvement Association. There were about a half dozen of us working out of that office and our task was to visit the member dairy farms in the area where we would be present for both morning and evening milking times. We would record the pounds of milk taken from each cow, take a sample, and deliver that to the main office that evening. The purity and percentage of butterfat content would be computed to give the dairy farm a one to five-star rating which, in turn, the creameries would pay more for the milk from the higher rated farms.

The job was a bit hard on the social life since you had to be at the farm usually by 4 a.m. and take your samples in after the evening milking. There were a few hours break in late morning and early afternoon that were usually spent parked under a shade tree taking a nap.

One of the dairy farms was so large that they had crews milking the cows 24-hours a day. We usually divided our crew in half and worked two cycles until we had two samples from each cow. On my crew there were two of us young guys and one older man who had retired years earlier, but liked this job as something to keep him busy. For the most part, he was a pretty grumpy old guy with no teeth who had a very limited vocabulary, most of which were foul and graphic swear words.

On one of the midnight shifts, the milking crew let in six cows to the milking parlor at a time. We were all standing in a pit so the cows' faucets were about chest high. One of the cows in the stantion nearest the steps was a young cow that had recently had a calf so she was a little jumpy. She was marked to alert the milking crew not to allow her milk to be put into the pipeline with that of the others. As cows are prone to do, she had just made a big mess on the floor of what cows do a lot of. At that moment, our foul-mouthed co-worker started down the steps which spooked the cow causing it to jump around some. One of the cows back hoofs hit that steaming pile of guess what sending a big glob of it flying through the air, landing with a big splat right in the mouth of the county cussing champion. We laughed so hard it hurt while he spit and cussed for the next hour. Was that poetic justice or what? And that Bible verse about "reaping what you sow" seems to apply here.

OK...for the squeamish, non-farmers among my readers, I'll move on to less "earthy" subjects. But, to answer a question I posed earlier about who flung dung...in this case, the cow did it!

Chapter II

Gerry Riggin' (or is it Jury Riggin')*

*The dictionary says either spelling is acceptable

My dad had a reputation around Lyman for being able to fix almost anything. He figured that if somebody could build it, he could find a way to fix it. His collection of old coffee cans in the garage filled with nuts, bolts, washers, screws, and miscellaneous pieces of thingamajigs of unknown origin testified to his confidence that they would be just the ticket for something that needed fixing. Most of the lamps in our house were rescued from the town dump and made as good as new by his skilled hands. My first bicycle arrived from the same source. I should add that my dad's ability did a DNA generational skip and landed on my son, Dave.

Up River

Undoubtedly, one of my dad's finest gerry rigging masterminds was his homemade burglar alarm for his garage. Occasionally some of his tools would come up missing so he figured a bit of audio-visual deterrent was required to fix that problem.

First, he mounted some floodlights that were activated by a motion sensor on the garage wall. Occasionally a stray dog, cat or raccoon would set it off and hightail it elsewhere in a hurry.

The best part of his system was that in the rafters inside the garage, he had mounted an old teardrop shaped (Eureka I think) vacuum cleaner (bought our mom a new fancy Kirby) that sucked air in one end and blew air out the back end with enough force to drive the fan of an old air-driven siren that he'd scavenged off an old retired fire engine. A relay switch would turn on that contraption at the same time the floodlights came blazing to life. The whole thing created a huge racket that sounded like one of those old air raid sirens that wailed when the enemy bombers would approach London (at least that is the way they sounded in the movies). I don't remember him saying that any more tools disappeared after that.

I don't think there is a Bible verse that actually says that, "one man's junk is another man's treasure," but in my dad's case, it is the gospel truth!

Chapter 12

Pop Goes Steelheading

I always enjoyed writing as was evidenced by an early postcard my mom saved that I had written from summer camp when I was probably 9 or 10. It said:

> "Dear Ma and Pa- How are you? I am fine. It
> pord (*poured*). Stanley puked on my pillow.
> Love, Me"

As you can see, I adhered to that old saying that is generally attributed to Mark Twain, "It is a poor and uncreative mind that can't find more than one way to spell a word."

However, I kept at it and will include a sample. It is a sing-songy poem written in Junior High about fishing.

Pop Goes Steelheading

Long before the crack of dawn
The bacon, eggs, and coffee are on.
The morning air bearing these wonderful smells
Gives an idea where a fisherman dwells.

Up River

A piping hot breakfast is first on his list
He certainly will need it; the cold to resist.
The wind and the weather he carefully considers
For there's no place around as cold as the river.

Remember the long-johns, we can't forget those
For they are an important part of a fisherman's clothes.
Along with his pipe, his coffee and pole
He sets out in a hurry for the old fishing hole.

His eagerness for fishing is exceedingly hot
And woe to the man that gets his favorite spot.
He carefully surveys his assortment of baits
Then throws out his line and patiently waits.

The wait is a long one, his patience grows thin
He longs for that battle he hopes he will win.
His nose and his toes agree that it's cold
He's hoping that big one will soon become bold.

Then suddenly! It hits with such fury and power
He knows that the battle will last a full hour.
The fish is a game one, it darts here and there
And every so often it leaps in the air.

A crowd gathers round to guess at the size
Of this ardent fisherman's well-deserved prize.
More than once it came close to the gaff hook in hand
But the fish was not anxious to swim on dry land.

So off he would dash with all of his might
"Til finally he had no more power to fight.

Then in he came slowly with an air of defeat
And turned on his back at the fisherman's feet.

The fisherman goes home with a feeling of pride
As his mouth is now watering to taste his fish fried.
But to this story there is never an end
For cracks the next dawn, there Pop goes again."

Wayne Coggins

Chapter 13

The Zone

Seventeen inches. That was/is the width of home plate in baseball, and that was the compass point in my life that motivated me to throw, throw, and throw some more so that, hopefully, I could hit the catcher's mitt as often as possible. In our Coggins' home movies are repeated scenes of me throwing something at something.

The river near our house offered me plenty of ammo for throwing. There were flat rocks for skipping and round ones for tossing a stick in the current and trying to hit it as it floated downstream.

In our orchard in the backyard there was one apple tree that was absolutely prolific with the amount of apples it produced. In fact, the fruit would hang so thick and heavy that Dad would often prop up some of the limbs with long poles to keep them from breaking. The problem was, the apples on this tree which we called a "sweet apple tree," were not at all good for eating. The apples were mushy and granular inside when they got ripe. So, we used them as food for the cows and pigs.

I used those sweet apples as wanna-be baseballs and would chuck them at fence posts. The cow pasture was on the south side and the pig pen to the north. When I was successful in hitting a post, the apple would shatter into pieces for the critters who would gobble them up. When I missed, they'd just run to where it landed and eat it whole. By the time the tree and the ground under it were empty, I could hit the fence posts most of the time.

Where I probably spent most of my time practicing when school was not in session, was behind the school where there was a blank wall on which I had used a crayon to draw a rectangular strike zone. It was exactly 17 inches wide and about 3 feet tall, and it was about the right distance from the wall to the playground fence. I had found a rubber ball that had seams like a regular baseball and was about the right weight.

I spent hour after hour pitching to my imaginary opposition which happened to be the line-up of the New York Yankees. Countless times (in my mind), I'd have the bases loaded and would strike out Mickey Mantle, Roger Maris, or Yogi Berra. Of course, the imaginary crowd would cheer, and I would walk off the field of battle (home), the victor.

The problem was, in reality, once I got the chance to pitch to real batters with a bat in their hands, and with real people watching, I'd get all nervous and sometimes that "17 inch zone" would get elusive and hard to find. I read somewhere recently that "worry is a waste of the imagination." I agree and, as a kid, I found a better use for mine.

Chapter 14

Grounded!

"You're grounded!" I think as a young teenager, I heard those dreaded words so often there is probably still a part of my brain where a "you're grounded" tattoo still remains. I think I was a classic slow learner when it came to obedience.

When I was younger, the ultimate teaching tool was to deprive me of my beloved BB gun for a day or a week or eternity (2 weeks). Or, if the offense was deemed serious enough, a trip to the woodshed would happen. I remember getting five spankings from my dad and most all of them involved that pesky BB gun. My mom, however, administered countless spankings usually with an apple tree switch. Oh, those things stung!

Then, in high school when I was finally able to drive myself, for some reason I had a hearing defect when my mom decreed the exact time I needed to pull in the driveway. 12 O'clock midnight somehow registered in my teenage brain as 12:45 or later. So, when I'd pull in the driveway, bound up the steps and open the door, there would be Mom standing next to the old Quaker oil-burning stove in her flannel nightgown with a "you're in trouble buster" look on her face. My excuses, though perfectly rational and legitimate to me, never held water with her. Sometimes I'd try to wrangle my way out of trouble with smooth talk, charming cuteness, humor, or pure baloney, but I'd cringe when she'd tell me to hush up and get to bed because I was grounded for the next week, ten days, or two weeks.

By the time I made it up the stairs to my room, I was already planning my strategy on how I'd whine and snivel my way into getting my sentence reduced. The next morning, as I'd begin to activate my plan, I'd hear the follow up judgment and sentence for my lateness. "Oh, by the way, since you're grounded, you will need to paint the fence posts and rails, the chicken house, or the barn, whichever was next in line from the last time I had painting punishment. I lacked the finesse and trickery of Tom Sawyer of Huckleberry Finn fame to convince my siblings, cousins, or friends to join me in the great fun of painting.

Occasionally, on rare occasions, my mom would give me a break and relent by reducing my time limit but, rather than it being mercy, I think she was just getting weary of my moaning, groaning, and pouting in my misery. Always though, and I mean always, she'd have us synchronize our watches before the keys to the family 1954 Chevy left her hands for mine. Then she'd ask me for my definition of what 12 midnight meant. 12 meant 12!

Most of a lifetime later, and after helping to raise three teenagers, there are three lessons that remain from those early experiences.

1. Most parents can't really sleep until all the chicks are in the nest.
2. There isn't really anything to do after midnight that is good.
3. To this day, I still hate to paint!

Chapter 15

Zeke and Hermie And the Westside Grocery

Our house was just inside the city limits on the west side of town on the old Lyman-Hamilton Highway. Our driveway was about 100 yards long, and at the beginning of it was the Westside Grocery, a local mom and pop store, that also sported regular and high-test Texaco gas pumps out front. These were the old-fashioned kind with a big glass see-through tank that would fill with gasoline before it would travel down the hose and into a car or truck. It was like a scene from an old Norman Rockwell painting, complete with an old bench out front in the shade where the old timers or us kids would sit and enjoy an RC Cola, Hire's Root Beer or a fast melting ice cream bar.

The store, at one time, had belonged to my mom during World War II, but before the war was over, she sold it to Zeke and

Hermie Holden, the sweet old couple who lived right next door. Zeke, whose real name was Joseph Alonzo, was the song leader at our church, and they were both much loved by the people in Lyman.

These were the days when people actually trusted each other and, if Mom was fixing dinner and discovered she needed something for a recipe, she'd send one of us kids out to the end of the driveway to the store where we would just say, "Charge it to Dad." Zeke or Hermie would pull a note card out of a little box and write down what we had bought. On the first of the month when my dad got paid, Mom would faithfully walk out to the store and settle up our account. While we grew most of our own food, and raised our own beef, pork, and chickens, I remember hearing my mom say that it cost about $100 worth of "store bought" food each month to feed our family.

It was always fun to watch Zeke or Hermie use their adjustable circular slicer to trim off a pound of baloney, ham, or bacon. The most fun though was looking out the back window where they had built a screened enclosure in which were two Eastern Gray Squirrels that they had imported from the mountains of Tennessee. Those energetic critters would spend hour after hour running as fast as they could on a big wire mesh wheel, going nowhere, but going there as fast as their little legs could take them.

We were never allowed to feed them because Zeke said they tended to be a little cranky and could easily mistake a kid's finger for a peanut treat. We did, however, get dizzy watching them go around and around on that wheel.

In later life I have often thought about that scene, watching those squirrels go in circles. There is a life lesson there to be sure. It is easy to get on the treadmill of life, get weary and go…nowhere. Motion without direction takes you exactly, nowhere.

Chapter 16

Blue Birds and the Oil Barrel Bong!

(Early lessons in the value of honesty)

It was the dog days of summer in our little town…those lazy days in a farming community after the berries and hay were harvested and the sweet corn and apples were nearing their prime. Most of us young school boys spent a lot of time at our favorite fishing spots or playing games like hide and seek in the twilight and often, on into the night. It was not unusual to have a half dozen or so boys spend the night sleeping under the stars in someone's backyard and we would sometimes have the added fun running around the neighborhood in just our tennis shoes and "tighty-whities" underwear just so we could brag about having been brave enough to actually do it.

The ultimate, however, was when someone would suggest that we have a game of "slingshot" war. We'd choose up sides and the ammo for our homemade slingshots was a couple of pockets full of rock-hard crabapples that were about the size of a ping pong ball. We'd sneak through the local alder and cedar patches to try to ambush the enemy troops with the rule of engagement being that the only legal "hit" was an enemy soldier's rear end. Believe me, the word "sting" had real meaning if you were the victim. Once hit, you had to go to the prearranged POW camp while the survivors continued with the war.

Well, it was one of those sweltry August days when all the "gang" seemed to be gone on family vacations and the only guys left to get into mischief were my cousin, Terry, and me. With not much to occupy our time, we came up with a grand plan to harass one of the local neighbors who had a large heating oil barrel beside the back door of their house which was beside the elementary school and seemed to invite being hit by a grenade (actually, an apple). We filled our pockets with ammo and snuck through the high grass to within range of our target and let loose with our first volley. Bong! Bong! came the deep echo as our grenades found their target. From our hiding place in the high grass we overcame our laughter long enough to peek at the door to see Oney (pronounced Awnie) Jackson poke out his angry head to see what was going on.

Moments after he went back inside, we let go with volley number two which caused another set of loud bongs to reverberate around the neighborhood, followed by another angry looking examination by Mr. Jackson (actually a very nice man). After we composed ourselves, we fired volley number three, not realizing that Mr. Jackson had left the screen door to his porch and his back door to the house wide open. To my shock, my next apple grenade soared wide to the right and went through the open screen door, through the back door and on through the length of their house and bounced off the inside of their front door. Standing there gawking at what had just happened, I wasn't quick enough to duck out of sight before Mr. J got a sure-fire glimpse of his little terrorist. Terry had disappeared somehow.

Later that evening when my dad got home from work, he came out to the orchard where I had been hiding in serious fear as to what fate might await me. Walking out to the orchard before he changed into his farming clothes told me I was in deep trouble. "Son," he said in his quiet but firm manner, "I think you'd better go have a talk with Mr. Jackson, don't you?" With my voice cracking under the stress, I replied, "What for?" All it took was a look, no words, and I knew there was no avoiding what had to be done. It was time to own up to my deeds of folly, be honest and apologize.

The two-block walk to the Jacksons seemed like "the longest mile" I could remember. When I came in sight of their house, there parked in front of it was the local police car…empty. My instincts told me to run for the hills because now, I KNEW I was in very deep trouble. But, running was not an option since Dad was at home waiting for my report. So, trembling like a fall maple leaf in the wind, I approached the back door, took a deep breath, and knocked quietly. Time seemed to stand still until finally the door creaked open and there stood, not Mr. Jackson but his tiny wife (maybe 4'8"), Hattie, looking as stern as a cranky school teacher on a bad day. Staring at my feet I managed to squeak out, "I'm sorry," fully expecting her husband and the town cop to reach around her, handcuff me, and lead me off to jail. Instead, she just reached out, lifted my shame-lowered head and said, "That's OK Wayne, just don't do it again." Relieved beyond words, I headed home, not knowing what further discipline awaited. When I saw my waiting dad, instead of a trip to the woodshed for a spanking, he just asked me what I had learned from my experience. (I was not aware that they had conspired to have the police car there for added reinforcement of my lesson.) Listening to my tearful explanation and my joy at being forgiven by Mrs. Jackson must have been a challenge for my dad to keep a straight face. Then, to my elation, instead of a whipping I well deserved, he said, " Let's go pick some fresh corn for supper."

The lessons here ...obviously, one is that having fun at someone else's expense just isn't a good thing. And, two, when you make a mistake and are tempted to try to weasel out of admitting and apologizing for it, it is important to realize that unresolved guilt is a much harder taskmaster than just owning up to it and making it right. The Bible says in Proverbs 28:13 that he who hides his mistakes pays a big price but the person who admits them finds mercy and gets another chance. What an offer!

Epilogue

Learning the value of honesty is a lesson that was reinforced that very next spring. Out of bb's for my trusty air rifle, and being flat broke, I contrived a plan to come up with a nickel to take care of my need.

Earlier that spring, our school had participated in a fund-raising project for the Children's Orthopedic Hospital in Seattle by having us school kids go door to door selling little cardboard "bluebirds" to folks. Well, I knew my mom had bought several so I took one and headed for our neighbors, Archie and "Delphie" Angel, to see if I could peddle it for a nickel. Turning on my best salesmanship, I was successful and before long my air rifle was full of bb's. I was in high clover having fun until my mom called me to come home. Her stern look told me that I had been found out. Another agonizing apology ensued followed up by that dreaded trip to the woodshed. Even worse was that my parents confiscated my bb gun for eternity (well, for two weeks anyway). Believe me, that old adage that crime doesn't pay, is the truth!

Chapter 17

The Dinner Table

There were some things that served as anchors for our lives growing up in a small town in the '50s and '60s. Besides church and God, school, sports, and neighborhood activities, there was the family dinner table where the whole family would sit down for the evening meal together. It provided the chance for everyone to share time, food, and our lives on a daily basis without any electronic interruptions. We'd share about our ups and downs, joys and dilemmas, as each person had a chance to add their own things to the mix.

At our house, dinner was usually between 5:30 and 6:00 pm most nights. It wasn't set in stone as sometimes a late sports practice or a game would cause a delay, or, in the summer, we might have to work later. Regardless, we always enjoyed and looked forward to dinner around the table. Did we appreciate that gathering as much then as we do now in retrospect? I doubt it. It was just the way life was.

If there was good news about an accomplishment, that was

shared. If someone was worried about an upcoming test, words of encouragement were offered. If one was in need of a piece of sports equipment or clothing, that was put out there and all eyes would turn to mom or dad to find out if the family budget could afford it. If the use of the family car was needed, a discussion of priorities or alternatives was talked over. Every so often a grievance would arise and usually some resolution; apology and forgiveness would occur. If a budding romance was faltering, words of comfort were shared or some coaching would happen. Seriously, that dinner time together was important to all of us kids as well as to Mom and Dad. It was one touchstone that caused everyone to feel that we were FAMILY.

Oh, there was regular good-natured teasing, especially from our dad who had refined that practice to an advanced art form, but it was Mom who came up with a good one on me one evening. The dinner ritual was basically that we all had our assigned places where we sat and everyone was supposed to wait until all were seated and the blessing spoken before we would begin to eat. I'd have to plead guilty to fudging a little on that protocol if I were really thirsty and would sometimes have a big gulp of the ice-cold milk sitting beside my plate. Well, my mom figured out a way of breaking that habit, so instead of the usual big glass of milk from our cow in front of me, she put a surprise in my glass. As I often did, I tried to snitch a swallow but instantly realized that something was seriously wrong…it was buttermilk! Yuk! I guess everyone else was in on the joke as they all broke into laughter as I ran to the kitchen sink to spit that nasty stuff out and rinse that taste out of my mouth. Lesson taught and lesson learned.

It kind of snuck up on the American family in the fifties when television came along and TV dinners were introduced. Sometimes a television set was brought into view of the dinner table to distract everyone, or plates were taken to the living room to be eaten from (you guessed it) TV trays. The sad bottom line is that gradually the conversations stopped and that sense of family connection and sharing sadly began to diminish. A few snatches of sharing during commercial breaks just didn't cut it.

Now (several decades later) it is often the case that many family members are only passing each other at laser speed, eating fast food in the car, or nobody is talking because earbuds are in their ears or video games or smart phones are captivating everyone's attention as they grab a slice or two of pizza and head to their room to eat while playing a video game or cruising through social media entries. I think there are generations of young folks that don't even know what they are missing.

Here in Alaska where we live, every now and then the power gets knocked out and all of the electronic devices that require an internet signal are dead. This causes all kinds of anxiety, boredom, and mayhem when families are suddenly forced to sit in a room and talk to each other. At the risk of some editorializing a bit, I would like to suggest that as moms and dads, kids, grandpas and grandmas, and adult siblings, we at least start sitting down together and enjoying the FAMILY DINNER TABLE and reconnecting as families -NOW- instead of needing a power outage or other calamity to force it to happen. I know that times change and it is not possible to turn back the calendar to the fifties, but re-establishing the family dinner table would be well worth the effort. Amen!

Chapter 18

My Thinkin' Tree

North of our house maybe a half-mile or so, across a pasture and a couple of barbed wire fences, lay the land of high adventure for a kid like me. Surrounded on the south end by a grove of old cedars and maples was the old Lyman Swamp. It ran east and west maybe a mile and was, perhaps, 10 feet deep at its deepest spot.

Occasionally, during a cold snap in the winter it might freeze over with 3-4 inches of crystal-clear ice. Lying on the ice and peering into the underwater world below it was, indeed, fascinating to discover all sorts of bugs and critters.

In the spring, one could pole an old fence-post raft out into the water and look down at the long jelly-like clusters of frog eggs with those embryonic little tadpoles in their early stages of development. This was Biology 101 before I could spell the word. Later in the spring and early summer when those little tadpoles morphed into opera stars, the evening quiet would be interrupted with a cacophony of frogs serenading the whole town. Once it warmed up enough at night, I'd tie a rope between a prune tree and an apple tree and throw a blanket over it to make a tent. Lying beneath it with my head out, I would stare up at the Milky Way and frequent shooting stars streaking across the sky and be lulled to sleep by those yodeling frogs.

Now, back to the swamp. My most sacred spot there was a huge maple tree that was probably 50-60 feet tall and 5-6 feet thick. About 5 feet up from the ground a huge branch jutted out about 10 feet before it curved up forming an "L" shape. The "L" actually extended out over the water, and if I stayed quiet and still, colorful ducks would swim under the limb, oblivious to my presence. It was my secret place to escape when I needed to think or daydream about life in my adolescent world. Sometimes, deep in thought, I'd doze off to sleep on my secret perch. The solitude and silence enabled me to dream big dreams and decide what life values were important to me. I learned to pray in the "L" of my old maple tree.

As the years flew by, the State built a new highway about 50 yards or so from my hideaway and the pastures were sold and subdivided. A visit to my sanctuary spot in my high school years found the tree still standing but it had died and was covered with moss. I considered climbing up to my old spot for some quiet contemplation when I noticed that a knot hole in the tree was a-buzz with hornets going in and out. So much for that idea.

A few years later on one of my visits back home from college, I stopped by that spot and discovered that my special tree had succumbed to the elements and had toppled over into the swamp. My thinkin' tree was gone but, over the years as an adult, wherever I have lived, I sought out a special place where I could sit, rest, think, and pray.

I didn't ever think to take a picture of that old tree by the swamp but I described it to an artist friend and this is her rendition on the next page.

Sketch by Kathy Loveland

Chapter 19

The Agony of De-feet!

I can't help it! That is, I can't help it that I was born with high arches and wide, relatively ugly feet. Not that I have ever figured that anyone's feet were all that good looking, but in our family the men have all inherited some especially ugly feet. On my birth certificate there is an imprint of my little foot and all that showed up was the ball of my foot and the heel. That's it. Some people have flat feet, but to picture mine, think the opposite.

I remember my mom taking me to a podiatrist once to see what they might be able to do to fix my feet. One suggestion was to break all the bones in my feet and reset them. I voted no on that, and, thankfully, my mom did too. What I ended up with were these ugly metal arch supports that fit inside my shoes which, for a kid, were very embarrassing.

I still have vivid memories of a swimming date in high school and the girl took one look at my feet, grimaced in surprise, and asked, "ooooh, do they hurt?" Then one day a girl asked me to accompany her to a youth group roller skating party (a few miles east of Lyman) at the Hamilton Roller Rink, known area wide for the "Wild Waves" feature along one wall with dips and valleys similar to a roller coaster. Skaters with the courage to "ride the waves" would sometimes be hauled off to the hospital with a broken arm or wrist.

As for me, I had never been on roller skates and could not find rental skates that were wide enough for my ten and a half EEEE width feet. So, I settled for a pair at least 3-4 sizes too big. Already shy and self-conscious, this was not going well so far.

Roller skating looked so effortless for those who have mastered the skill. Even little kids could do it, so surely I could too. I soon discovered that it was not as easy as it looked. Out on the rink we went to the tune of "Shake, Rattle and Roll" with me in tow behind my date, hanging on to her waist for dear life. I don't think I ever went for more than ten feet when, "bam," down I went crashing to the floor, ungracefully, on my rear end! After a while, the girl finally gave up on me and left me clinging to the side wall, inching my way embarrassed, to the opening where there was a bench where I could sit and sulk in my "agony of defeat."

I suppose most young kids have experienced similar horrifying failures at which time we often make powerful inner vows about that moment. Mine was, "I will NEVER subject myself to that kind of humiliation again!" That is one vow I have never been even remotely tempted to break. These feet of mine are pretty good for walking, but for skating…no way! One thing for sure, those experiences gave me a keen sense of empathy for people who struggle with various things that are difficult for them but seemingly effortless for others.

Chapter 20

The Bees and Me

When I see one of those pictures in a magazine or on-line of a person covered with bees, seemingly calm, cool, and collected, it makes me cringe! While I am not one of those unfortunate people who are allergic to bee stings, I still harbor memories of childhood bee encounters and would never want to have a pet bee named Bob as a buddy.

One warm summer morning when I was twelve or so, I was riding my old bike home from checking the mail when a bumblebee the size of a jaw breaker flew down my shirt and before I could get it out of there, it stung me right on one of those two seemingly useless bumps on either side of my chest. Those were sensitive spots about that stage of life so let's just say it was serious pain! I immediately stood up on the bike pedals to hurry home so my mom could put something on the wound to make the pain go away. But right then the chain on my bike slipped off the sprocket and I came crashing down astride the bike frame crossbar with a take-your breath-away blow to yet another vulnerable area! I wobbled to a stop and distinctly remember saying out loud, "I'm having a really bad day!!!" To this day, I blame it all on that bumblebee.

Later that summer, a couple of my cousins, some neighborhood friends, and I went on a hike across the swamp along a ridge that ran north of our house to see what adventures we might encounter. At some point one of the game trails we followed opened up to a clearing where we spotted an old shed. With a little effort the old door swung open on its rusty hinges revealing a bunch of old leather horse harnesses. It was a treasure trove as we checked it all out imagining the old days when loggers and farmers used horses and mules to get the heavy work done.

What we did not notice was the football-sized hornet's nest hanging from the low rafters that my tall cousin Terry's cowboy hat was bumping when he turned from side to side. We didn't notice that until that little shack suddenly filled with angry and aggressive hornets bent on driving us intruders from their territory. All five of us hit that door at the same time, but being the smallest, I was the last one out. I got nailed with seven stings that felt like they were on fire. My dislike for any species of the bee family grew exponentially that day.

Among his many interests, my dad was a bee keeper and we usually had a hive or two out back between the barn and the chicken house. We often had a square of honey in the comb on our breakfast table that we all enjoyed. When it came time to rob the bees of some of their honey, my dad would don a head net and use a smoke producing can which seemed to keep the bees from stinging him. Bee keeping was never a hobby I aspired to have.

I have vivid memories of being out in a strawberry patch picking berries in early summer when some nearby bees would swarm and hundreds or probably thousands of the critters would pass over us looking for a new place to call home. The field boss had instructed the picking crew, if that happened, the bees would not bother us if we just lie down and stay still between the rows. It worked, but it sure was hard not to bolt and run when the sound of that mass of bees was buzzing all around you.

Later in life, my brother decided to keep some bees and sell the honey as a family project. They also acquired a small herd of tiny goats to rent out to people who wanted to get rid of some unwanted blackberry bushes. Those little critters would eat those thorny bushes right down to the dirt. I thought the name of their family business was pretty clever. Taking off from a popular breakfast cereal at the time, they called it, "Honey Bunches of Goats."

Not to miss a chance to use a Biblical metaphor, the Bible says that on one occasion, the army of the Israelites went against God's instructions and stormed a city with the results that the enemy came out and "chased them as bees do!" I think I know a little of how that must have felt.

Chapter 21

Puzzles

As I was growing up, holidays were always pretty special times. I have several Zip-Lock bags of pictures and one old very long VHS tape compiled from 8mm film taken by Mom and Dad that captured some of the cast of characters that shared those special days with our family. Grandparents, uncles and aunts, cousins and family friends are all there. Sadly, many of them are no longer alive and are missed dearly.

July 4th was always fun since our area had an annual celebration referred to as the Logger-Rodeo. Logging had been a mainstay of the local economy for years so they celebrated that history with a popular parade, a carnival, some logging skill events, and a two-day rodeo at the old dilapidated rodeo grounds at the edge of town (Sedro Woolley). There are pictures of yours truly, along with my other teammates from the Lyman Hamilton Loggers little league team, waving at my dad with his old movie camera as we rode in the parade, hanging on to the cab of a fully loaded logging truck. Years later, there is some footage of me marching in the high school band in our snappy blue uniforms and hats and white shoes. It is hard to believe I was ever that young and certainly ever that slim!

However, the most repeated segments in those old home movies are the Coggins' Family Christmas gatherings. Each one begins with a shot of an old chalk board with the year written on it for the sake of history. Then the camera pans around the old farmhouse living room zooming in on the faces of the family and friends gathered for sharing the joys of giving and receiving the gifts of love for one another. It was fun to watch which ones were careful to open their gifts so the paper, ribbons and bows could be used again next year and which of us just ripped the paper to shreds. Both approaches revealed a bit of the personalities of the recipients or a bit of the story of their lives that had been impacted by the Great Depression of the 1930's or other hard times.

After all the hoopla and a huge dinner that was enjoyed by all, the next event was an obligatory afternoon nap on anything soft, warm and inviting. Well, at least that is what all the adults did. As the mellow afternoon blended into the early evening, and while cold turkey sandwiches from the leftovers began appearing, so did another great tradition – THE ANNUAL JIGSAW PUZZLE! Perhaps it was a new one or a favorite from years gone by but it got spread out on a table or countertop and the whole family took turns at the four corners of the project looking for the edge pieces and then the frustrating process of trying to find just the right piece for your end of the puzzle which was somewhere in the middle of another 1000 or so other pieces that looked almost identical to the one you were trying to locate. The amount of patience and endurance shown by different co-laborers also gave a glimpse into their unique personalities and traits. It usually took several days to complete the miserable thing, and it was often one or two die-hards that finally would let out a victory whoop when the last piece was put in place.

Looking back on those family puzzle gatherings most of a lifetime later, I have realized that it wasn't about that crazy puzzle at all. The puzzle was something that simply drew our family together in close enough proximity and for a long enough period of time for us to stay connected with each other. Family stories and history were shared. Problems or future plans had a way of spilling out. Probably an old grudge or two got aired out and forgiven and more than a few hugs were given with words of love and encouragement…all becoming a part of the fabric that makes family…family.

CHAPTER 22

The Russians are Coming

It was 1962 and I was 16 years old when President Kennedy squared off politically and militarily with the Soviet Union and its leader, Nikita Kruschev. The United States had discovered that Russian missiles were being deployed to Cuba, a mere 103 miles from Florida and US soil. It was a 13-day extremely tense time with the two super powers teetering on the brink of a potential nuclear war. Thankfully, the Russians backed down and calmer days ensued.

That was not the case in our little part of America where my dad was a civil defense coordinator for our county. We were busy constructing a bonafide fallout shelter in our side yard where once stood a huge old black cherry tree. We had dug into a slope making room for a foundation about 20x20 feet. Prior to laying the foundation, we had dug a well and sunk a sand point into a good water supply with the well pipe extending out of the ground inside the future shelter site.

I remember my dad installed a grid of re-bar (reinforcing

bar) and instructed me to wrap soft wire around all of the junction spots. It was hard work with lots of bending over and occasional skinned knuckles. Later, I remember I was the official cement block carrier and mortar mixer while my dad was putting up the walls. When I say that "we" built the shelter, it was kind of like holding the ladder while an artist painted a mural, and then getting to pose for a picture with the artist and the mural "we" painted.

After the walls were up to ground level, we put a thick concrete slab on the top (more re-bar), allowing for an entrance and a stairway down inside the shelter. On top of that, Dad built a small room that served as an efficiency apartment where my grandpa lived for several years.

I remember the basement shelter had a flush toilet, a small lead-lined window, an air filtration system, and a manual pitcher pump. Inside, there were bunk beds for our family and the walls were lined with shelves, which in later years served as storage for canned food. I recall there was also one or two 55-gallon drums in which was a radiation detector and various packages of food including some fairly tasty "survival crackers."

For years, after the crisis with Russia was in the rear-view mirror, if Mom was fixing dinner and needed a jar of pickles or green beans, she sent one of us scampering down into that shelter to retrieve them for her. In 2018, my wife and my siblings were granted permission to visit the old (now remodeled) farmhouse in Lyman. That old cement block shelter and apartment atop it were still standing.

I always admired my dad's knowledge of building and providing for his family just in case a disaster might have struck, but I don't think he was overly thrilled when a local newspaper ran a feature story, complete with pictures, of the shelter. Now that everyone in the county knew where a fully functional fallout shelter was located, it would become anything but a safe haven with folks desperate to get in there. But then, that was the 60s and the cold war with Russia was in full swing.

Psalm 91 seems appropriate to mention here. While there are examples of preparing for impending disasters (The Ark, famine preparation, etc.), it is good to remember that dwelling in the "secret place of the Most High" should not to be overlooked.

In retrospect, as I look back on those long hours of hard work building that shelter, the blessing of working with, and time spent, with my dad are priceless memories.

Chapter 23

High School Hazards

Miss Grandadam was one of my favorite teachers in Sedro Woolley High School. She taught Spanish, which I found an enjoyable subject…right alongside of P.E., band, orchestra, and choir. An older single lady, I had discovered that she had a great fondness for the oatmeal chocolate chip cookies that my mom put in my lunch nearly every week. Regularly, Mom would put an extra baggie of them in my lunch for me to pass along to Miss Grandadam. She loved them, and I enjoyed seeing her smile. After all these years, I still remember some Spanish beyond taco, enchilada, and burrito.

One of the unwritten social expectations of a high school guy with a girlfriend in the 60s was that the boy would hustle out of his class as quick as the bell rang and run to the part of the building where his girlfriend's class was located to escort her and carry her books to her next class; then run like crazy to make it to his next class on time.

The classroom doors in the old section of the building were tall things, probably 7-8 feet high with the top half being that opaque, fuzzy glass, that let in some light, but you couldn't clearly see through it. One day, at the bell signaling the end of Spanish class, I made a break for the door, as my girlfriend's class was one story down and clear at the other end of the building. What I didn't know was that some prankster had removed the door pins from the hinges so when I opened the door, instead of it swinging open normally, it came crashing down to the floor with a loud noise, sending shattered glass all over the hallway. I stood there speechless, but Miss Grandadam was not. She figured I had run right through the door.

It didn't take long to figure out what had happened which got me off the hook. Thankfully, nobody was on the other side of the door because they surely would have been injured. From then on though, I'd gingerly test the door before making my high-speed run down the hall.

As far as I know, the culprit who stole the door pins never fessed up to his deed. However, I suspect he or she probably has those door pins in their high school memorabilia box and rehearses the story to their grandkids or at class reunions.

Chapter 24

Swapping Sandwiches

For all of junior high and most of high school I took my lunch to school in one of the standard brown paper bags that my mom bought by the bundle. My mom was an expert lunch fixer, and saw to it that I had several sandwiches, an apple or banana, and some of her famous chocolate chip oatmeal cookies. In high school, a group of us had our regular lunch table under the steps that led up to the teachers' lunch area. Sometimes we'd swap sandwiches if someone had a good-looking trade. My friend, Ivan, often had roast venison sandwiches in his lunch pail and we both enjoyed the trade for my tuna or egg salad.

Now and then, if Mom was not feeling too swift, she'd give me a couple of dollars to buy a lunch in the school cafeteria. There was one line for regular food and another for a hot dog or hamburger. Those hot dogs and burgers were good, and the girl dispensing them was pretty cute, even wearing the required hair net. So, hot dogs or hamburgers it was! The cafeteria cooks were always friendly and the food nutritious, but hominy and spinach never were in the top ten menu selections for most of us kids.

About my junior year, I discovered that if you could make it back to the school by the time the lunch hour was over, there was a Mom and Pop Café a few blocks away that catered mostly to upper classmen and specialized in hamburgers in a hurry. When you walked in you would hold up one or two fingers indicating a plain burger or a cheese burger. Within a minute or two your order was ready and they would deliver it to your table with a coke and bag of chips. That was fancy dining for a farm-raised high school kid.

I don't think the burgers were any better than the ones served in the cafeteria. It was just the cool place to go now and then. Mom and Pops was a place where the athletes and "cool" people would go and where us "wanna-be" jocks and nerds would aspire to be, in case some of that "cool" would rub off on us. Looking back, it was always a better deal eating with old friends that accepted you, while swapping for a venison sandwich with Ivan at our special table under the stairs.

Chapter 25

Growth Spurts

My September birthday almost caused me to have to wait another year to start first grade. But, since I would be six on the 10th, they decided to let me start school at age five. Quite a few of my classmates were almost a year older and a few clicks taller, and more coordinated, than I was. But I survived and, over time, it all evened out. In later family pictures I look a head taller than the rest of my siblings and my parents. We had a door jam between our kitchen and utility room where I had a mark and wrote in pencil, "six feet or bust." I made it.

Achieving my goal was not without its problems. It happened between 8th and 9th grades. That summer I hit a growth spurt and grew six inches in those three months. I was skinny as a bean pole and all of my jeans that I'd bought earlier in the summer were now "high water" and embarrassing to wear to school. Add to that, it was about that time that my voice decided to change and would skip an octave of its own accord, especially when I was trying to talk to a girl or had to give a speech in class.

To add to my misery, while I had been fairly coordinated as my shorter self, I became more than a little clumsy for quite a while. The problem culminated in some embarrassing moments in PE class. The gym teacher placed us all on basketball teams based on our ability to shoot and dribble. My friend, Kenny, and I found ourselves relegated to the illustrious 9th string. Oh, yippee! So, for the duration of our basketball classes, Kenny and I just wrestled around on the rolled-up mats and never got the chance to dribble or make a basket.

That is…until we were allowed to play a game they called Russian Basketball, which had no rules and everyone got to play at the same time. You could run with the ball, kick it, throw it; whatever it took to get it in the basket. Indeed, it was a rough and tumble game and was "shirts against the skins." (One side wore their t-shirts, the other no shirts)

I have an indelible memory of a time when there was a big dog-pile of about 20 guys all piled on one fairly chubby boy on the "skins" side who had the ball. Suddenly there was a blood-curdling scream from the bottom of the pile and the gym teacher intervened. When everyone un-piled, the fellow who'd had the ball said someone had bitten him. Nobody would fess up to the deed, but eventually the guilty boy sheepishly confessed and the teacher called a technical foul on him which, I think, included an apology to the victim and a few threatened swats from the teacher's paddle. Junior High could be dangerous!

Chapter 26

Piggins and Porkchop

I'm pretty certain that most of us remember that old adage that "Sticks and stones may break your bones, but names (or words) can never hurt you." You may also have had the experience of eating a bologna sandwich. What that old saying and the contents of that sandwich have in common is that both are...PURE BALONEY!

My Lyman memories are peppered with some of the nicknames that some of the older residents were known by. Some colorful ones were, Stoggie, Yuler, and Boogerman. I could name a few others but they would likely be considered "R" rated or too insulting to mention. My dad had a nickname that his old friend, Tate Kirkpatrick, gave him. It was "the jedge (judge)" based on my dad's skills as a mediator of neighborhood disputes.

I can remember some of my own nicknames that I had over the years. Jake Koops, who owned the Lyman Market, used to call me "Skidmore," the roots of which remain a mystery. I had quite a southern accent as a youngster so some of my relatives called me "Tarheel." My younger siblings called me "Bubber Wayne" and I am fairly certain my older sister referred to me as "The Pest" due to the creative pranks I delighted in pulling on her. Later in life, I was known as "Marrying Sam," Brudder Goggin," "The Love Doctor," and my grandkids called me "Papa Wayne," and later jokingly shortened it to "P.P. Wayne." One day I called my daughter, Tracie, and a man answered that I mistakenly thought was her husband, Darren. I said, "Hi, this is P.P. Wayne," to which he replied, "And this isn't Darren." Oh, brother!

The hurtful side of nicknames, especially when you are a young person, can have quite an effect on you. Being raised on a small farm just a few blocks from the Lyman Grade School, we raised a lot of our own food, including cows, chickens, and pigs. My dad had arranged with the school kitchen staff to have the clean-up crew scrape off the trays of uneaten food into a ten-gallon galvanized pail which would be set just outside the basement door for me to carry home after school to give to our pigs. Those critters would eat anything I'd bring home in that "slop bucket", and it saved my dad a considerable amount of money.

Every day I would carry that cleaned and empty bucket back to the school. That did not go unnoticed by one of my classmates who decided to do a spin-off of my last name. Instead of Coggins, he started calling me Piggins. Oh joy, to a bashful kid like me that was humiliating and embarrassing. In retaliation, I started calling him by his equally embarrassing nickname. A bit on the chubby side, he was occasionally called "Pork Chop".

One day, he and I got into an argument over something (stupid I am sure) and we started calling each other those nicknames, face to face. The result was that he challenged me to a fight just off the school grounds when school let out. News of an impending fight spread through that 5th and 6th class like wildfire. I don't think either of us had ever had a grudge fight before, but by then it was too late to back out.

We faced off at the street corner and were surrounded by classmates eager to see us go at it. Not knowing exactly how to go about it, he sneered and called me, Piggins. I retaliated by calling him Pork Chop. That began a half dozen or so exchanges of Piggins and Pork Chop. Then for some reason, both Piggins and Pork Chop started laughing at the absurdity of the situation and the crowd joined in the laughter as well. After that we all walked over to the nearby store to celebrate with an RC Cola and some peanuts.

When everyone dispersed, I walked back over to the school and picked up that pesky slop bucket and headed for home. Interestingly, neither of us ever used those nicknames again.

Chapter 27

Playing Hooky

I remember awakening early on my 73rd birthday and feeling profoundly thankful for the years I have been allowed to enjoy. As I was pondering some of my earliest childhood memories, a scene came to me that I had actually seen just the morning before. While sitting in my car at an intersection, waiting for the light to change, a big yellow school bus made a turn right in front of me. As it passed close-by, I could see that all of the seats were taken by little kids on their way to school. Most were barely tall enough to see out the windows, so my view looked like a bus full of little bobble-heads as the bus bounced along, taking them to week one or two of kindergarten.

After the bus had passed and I made my turn toward home, my thoughts had gone back to my first days of school at Lyman Grade School. With a September birthday, I started first grade while I was still five years old. Our house was just a few minutes from the school so I didn't need to ride a bus, but just carry my lunch pail across a neighbor's side yard, and I was there in a minute or two.

I was a shy little guy with freckles and a cowlick in my hair, and maybe a bit smaller than some of my classmates with a few being almost a year older than I was. Our teacher, Mrs. Dinglefritz, (obviously not her real name) was usually pretty crabby and had a way of coming up behind a squirmy student and pinching them on the shoulder. It hurt. Being a left-handed person, I had her frequently at my desk trying to get me to either use my right hand or at least hold my pencil differently.

One day, as she was making her way toward me during our penmanship exercises, I knew I was in for a "pinch", so I quickly raised my hand and asked permission to go to the restroom. She grumpily granted the request, and I scooted out the door and across the hall to the boys' bathroom. I dawdled around in there for about five minutes and finally headed back to the classroom when, just outside the door, I heard an angry Mrs. Dinglefritz say, "Where is that Wayne Coggins? He's been gone too long and he is in trouble."

This was one of my first experiences of the "fight or flight" principle, and I chose the flight option. I slipped out a side door and ran all the way home where I burst through the door and gave what I thought was an academy award winning performance of being sick nigh unto death. When Mom asked me where I was hurting, I indicated that it hurt everywhere.

I think she wasn't fooled because there had been no call from the school nurse before I made my sick trip home. So, she called my bluff and sentenced me to spend the rest of the day in bed. I remember that it was a long, long boring afternoon that was probably worse than getting "the pinch." Besides that, I was in trouble for leaving school without permission and the next day I had to face the scowling Mrs. Dinglefritz.

I learned my lesson and through the rest of my school years never again yielded to the temptation to play hooky. Life lessons come our way early and often, and in my case, the Bible verse (Proverbs 28:13) that says that the person who admits their mistakes gets another chance seems to apply.

Chapter 28

Oops – Rapture

At the Lyman Mission Church, it was not unusual for the pastor or visiting evangelist to preach on "the rapture." That subject is taken from the Bible verses referring to the moment in time when God's hourglass has run out and those who have believed in Jesus will be "caught up" to be with Jesus for eternity. As big moments in the history of mankind go, this is the really big one.

After hearing those sermons either at church or summer camp, I had enough fear instilled in my mind that, to me, missing out on the rapture would be the ultimate OOPS moment for all time and eternity. Now and then, a preacher would dramatize this event and have us kids, who had bad thoughts or told a lie, streaming to the altar at the front of the church to repent and make sure we had sealed the deal with God, and had some assurance that if we got zapped by lightning or squashed by a truck on the way home from church, we'd be okay and wake up in heaven.

For all of my years in grade school, my mom was what they call today, a "stay at home mom." Dad worked at Northern State

Hospital and Mom worked at home raising us kids, keeping the flower beds and gardens weeded, and making sure we got to the dentist or doctor on time. Come what may, when school was out, a short walk home would always find Mom at home with a PB & J sandwich or some fresh-baked cookies for us to snack on to tide us over until about 5:30 when Dad would get home and it was supper time.

That was the case, except for one terrifying day when I got home from school, fully expecting to find Mom there as usual. "Mom" I called out. "Mom," I yelled a little louder. No answer. "Mom?" I hollered. "Mom, where are you?" I ran to all the rooms in the house and looked out back through the kitchen window. No Mom.

It was then that a ghastly fear gripped my mind that the rapture must have occurred and everybody else in the family had shot up into the sky toward heaven, and I had been left behind. In a panic, I ran to the front door and out on the porch and frantically looked up into the sky for maybe a sight of Mom and the others waiting and waving for me to come on up and join them.

I remember that I took a jump from the 3rd step up, hoping that gravity would let go and I'd soar up and join the rest of my family. Instead I landed with a thump, both feet hitting the sidewalk. I climbed back up the steps a couple of times and tried again with the same results. I was about to be overcome with terminal despair when I looked up and saw Mom walking up the driveway with a bag of groceries from the store out on the highway.

I can't describe the sweet sense of relief that I felt as I ran out to meet her and gave her a big hug. I doubt she ever had a clue as to why her son was so clingy for the rest of the evening.

Chapter 29

The Model A and the Unguided Rocket

Through most of the '50s and '60s we had two cars. One was the family car which I remember early on as an ugly Nash Rambler station wagon and later, a 1954 Chevy Belaire four-door that was the color of a rusty nail. Parked in the woodshed beside the garage was a 1933 Model-A Ford that my dad drove to work every day at the Northern State Hospital nine miles away in Sedro Woolley.

It seemed that people were regularly trying to buy that car from my dad, but he loved that old thing and wasn't about to sell it. He always kept a current edition of the JC Whitney auto parts catalog near his arm chair in the living room from which he could order parts for that old jalopy if something needed fixing. He used to joke that he could fix most anything on that car with bailing wire and a pair of pliers.

Up River

Several of my childhood memories included that old Model A. I remember that on occasion the battery would fail and my dad would reach under the front seat and would pull out a manual hand crank which he would insert into the front of the car to start it if it was being stubborn. If I were around, he would usually exhort me not to try that myself as sometimes the crank would "kick" back with enough force to break, or at least bruise an arm. Usually, after a few tries the car would start and chirp and putter out the driveway. I learned to operate the 3-speed manual floor transmission in that car long before I was old enough to get a learner's permit.

Some of my best memories in that car had to do with going fishing with my dad in it. There was one particularly good steelhead fishing spot that was only accessible by boat or by driving (with the owner's permission) across a pasture on a usually muddy and rutted road. The ruts were so deep that a regular car could get high centered on it, but the old Model-A tires made it high enough for clearance. I have a distinct memory of sitting in that car beside the river to get out of a rain squall, listening to the torrential rain beat a steady rhythm on the tar-covered roof, and my dad offering me coffee from his thermos to warm me up. Ugh! It was nasty tasting stuff.

Then, one year when I was ten or so, as the spring opening for lake fishing approached, Dad said that we would go up the valley (probably 25 miles away) to Grandy Lake and we'd sleep outside on the ground UNDER the Model A. Wow! Camping with Dad was about as good as it got, in my mind. Since we didn't have a boat then, there was a place where we could fish from shore if we could be the first ones there.

What we hadn't counted on was at some time in the night, a thunderstorm hit with thunder, lightning and a "gully washer" downpour of rain. Once the rain started to run in small streams under the car and into our sleeping bags, we clamored up into the car, turned the heater on high while the rain pelting the roof sounded like we were inside a tympani drum. The back seat was filled with our soggy sleeping bags so we spent the rest of a miserable night trying to get comfortable enough to sleep. By daylight, when it should have been time to fish, the rain was still coming down hard, so, stiff, sore, and hungry, we both figured that the best move was to head home fishless, but looking forward to a warm bath and some bacon and eggs.

Then in the fall of 1963, my junior year in high school, my physics class lab partner, John, and I had a class project where we were to make a rocket, fire it off, and record some sort of data about its flight. We got a metal tube, put a wooden point on it, glued some wings at the bottom, filled it with fuel, (sulphur I think) and without permission, drove that old Model A up Prevedel Hill to a big logged off field to our version of Cape Canaveral. We propped our unguided rocket up against an old stump, lit a magnesium strip fuse, and ran like crazy to hide behind another stump to watch it fly. All we got was a "pffttt" sound as the fuse ran out and nothing else happened. Disappointed, we headed back down that steep hill listening to the brakes screech and growl all the way down. That was when I remembered my dad saying the brakes were shot and were metal on metal.

When we got to my house, we piled up some old tires and rims, propped our rocket up against them, pointed it out our driveway, and lit a butane torch against the rocket's rear end and ducked around the corner. Suddenly that fuel ignited and the rocket went flying out the driveway a few feet off the ground until it veered off course and stuck in the back of Johnny Watson's woodshed where it fizzled out.

I think we basically had built something like a stick of dynamite that was open on one end. It didn't go off as originally planned because the fuel had oxidized. I think we got a "D" on the project, but were pretty fortunate that we hadn't started a forest fire or lost some body parts if that thing had exploded.

It turned out that in 1963, that 1933 Model A Ford turned 30 years-old and officially qualified as an antique car. That motivated my dad to finally sell that old relic. I remember he got $800 for it which was a pretty fair sum in that era. Later, I learned that one of the main reasons he had sold it was that he had directed me not to drive it with those bad brakes, a warning I had ignored. He sold it to make sure I didn't get killed driving that old rattle trap!

Chapter 30

Attic Monsters

When I was about five years old, my parents moved our family from Lyman's "uptown" neighborhood to an old run-down house with a few acres of land on the west side, just inside the city limits. To the north of our house was a gully that, I think, at one time was a channel or slough off the Skagit River. The ground was so fertile that you could turn the soil over, plant some seeds, and grow just about anything. Out in back of the house was an orchard with a number of types of apples, pears, plums, prunes, walnuts, and cherries. Blackberry bushes covered most of the fences. Fixing that place up kept our family busy for years.

When my dad remodeled the house, he partially finished the upstairs which became my room. The south end (my bedroom), was paneled and carpeted, but behind an old door with a wooden latch, was the dark and foreboding attic with its exposed rafters and a little catwalk so someone could walk to the north wall and open a window if some airflow was needed.

During those years, my dad worked at Northern State Hospital, which was about 9 miles to the west. This was a large mental hospital, and it was not uncommon for one or more patients to walk away from the grounds and head east toward Lyman. Sometimes they would find a house where no one was home and might go inside and see what was in the refrigerator. As a general rule, they were harmless, but if frightened or surprised, they might not react well. On occasion, a neighbor might spot someone who looked like they could be a patient walking along the road. They would call my dad who would drive over to the highway, pick them up, and bring them to our house for a sandwich. They most always recognized and felt safe around him. In the meantime, Mom would have called the hospital and soon a couple of orderlies would arrive at the house to give them a ride back to the safety and security of the hospital.

One warm summer evening when I was ten or so, our family had gone somewhere and didn't get home until it was dark and bedtime. So, up the stairs I went to my room to bed. I was almost asleep when suddenly I heard the attic door creaking open. Once, then twice. Being a kid with a big imagination, I instantly thought that one of those patients was hiding in the attic and was getting ready to come out, grab me, and do me in.

Hanging crossed on the wall by my bed were an old Japanese military sword and a scabbard that my dad had brought home from Okinawa after the war. The sword was actually pretty dull, but looked quite menacing. Scared half out of my wits, I decided to take action. With one hand I turned on my bedside lamp, and with the other I grabbed my weapon, and jumped out of bed with the sword ready to swing, and squeaked out, "come out of there or I'll cut your head off!" Nothing happened so I yelled it again. That was enough to bring my mom running up the stairs to see what the commotion was.

There I stood, armed and ready in my tighty whities, and I

blurted out that there was a crazy man in the attic. My mom, calm as could be, looked down and saw that the door latch was in the open position and began to laugh. It turned out that she realized it was going to be uncomfortably warm upstairs that night and she had gone up and opened the windows at both ends of the house and left the attic door open so the breeze would cool things down. There was a slight breeze which was causing the door to move and squeak on its hinges. My attic monster turned out to be the wind. My young heart was still thumping in my chest so that even though my mom shined a flashlight into that dark old attic to relieve my fears, I still had a hard time finally drifting off to sleep.

Psalm 91 says that when we dwell in the secret place of the Most High (God), we need not be afraid of the terror that comes at night. That is a comforting thought, but I still kept that sword handy just in case until I left for college and bequeathed both it and my bedroom to my brother, Mark.

Chapter 31

Make and Rindy

Grandpa's Front Porch

My dad's dad was indeed a colorful and interesting old man when I knew him. His real name was Malcolm, but everyone in our little town just knew him as, Make. His wife, Marinda, known by all as, Rindy, was a kind and sweet old Tennessee mountain woman that we were told was part Cherokee Indian. Most interestingly about her is that her maiden name was Messer and it is through that side of the family that our family became 5th cousins to Dolly Parton. Another limb in that family tree deserving mention was my great, great uncle (I think), Fredrick Messer, who lived his entire life in a cabin in the Smokey Mountains of Tennessee and lived until he was 114 years-old! I have an old newspaper story with a picture of him sitting on the porch of his cabin, holding his old black-powder musket, at the age of 104. He, by the way, is my role model for aging. Let's see, I'm 74 as I am writing today, so, if God was to grant me that wish, I'd have about 40 more years to go. Oh, my, I'd better keep flossing my teeth, and I wonder what life will be like if we make it until 2060.

As a boy, one of my favorite things to do was to walk the few blocks to Grandpa's house where I'd usually find him sitting in his front porch rocking chair, a cane across his lap, watching the occasional car go by. I'm not sure where his signature greeting came from, but he'd always say, "It's awful ain't it, Wayne?" I'd reply, "Yup Grandpa, it sure is." To which he'd reply, "Nah, it's worse than that." Then, he'd break into a toothless grin and commence rocking back and forth telling me of his life adventures. I was all ears and ate it all up as the gospel truth.

Several memories stick vividly in my mind of afternoons with my grandpa. He always had an old .22 caliber pistol on his lap. When I asked him if he was expecting robbers, he would say no but, being a serious diabetic, he said that if he ever got bitten by a dog, he'd probably get gangrene and die. Come to think of it, I never did see a dog venture into his yard. He also almost always had a wad of chewing tobacco in his jaw and, for the most part, he could hit his old coffee can spittoon. Like I said, he was a colorful character.

Another fun part of visits to Grandpa's house was watching him eat an apple. He loved them and my dad kept him well supplied from our orchard. If he had a pair of false teeth, I never saw him wear them, so eating an apple was tricky. He would have to wait until the apples were so ripe and mushy they were nearly rotten. Then, he'd squeeze and massage the pitiful apple until it was almost applesauce under the skin. Grandpa's face was wrinkled and thin and sported a rather prominent chin that jutted out quite a bit, and above that was a long beak of a nose, so that (minus teeth) when he'd chew (gum) an apple, his nose and chin would almost touch. Watching that whole process was more than worth the price of admission.

Grandpa's house was right across the street from the Lyman City Park which sported numerous picnic tables. One day, while I was sitting on the porch with Grandpa, a family of four pulled into the park for a picnic. The table was not designed for balance with angled legs, so when they sat down to eat, disaster struck. The papa picnicker was like the proverbial Jack Sprat and was skinny as a rail. Momma, however, was a very large woman, and the kids didn't register into the weight distribution equation. When momma sat down on her side, the table flipped up on his side and hit the grass on hers, sending potato salad, pork and beans, fried chicken, watermelon, and kids flying through the air. It seemed funny at first until I noticed that the mom and kids were all crying. These days I think they call that, "dark comedy." Laughter at someone else's expense really isn't all that funny. Grandpa and I both felt sad as that disappointed family salvaged what they could eat, piled in their car, and drove away.

Around Christmas of my senior year in high school, an ambulance rushed Grandpa to the hospital. He'd had a stroke. I spent many hours next to his bedside, hoping he would regain consciousness, but he never did.

To my knowledge, Grandpa had never made peace with God, and I kept pleading for him to squeeze my hand, blink, or anything to let me know that he had accepted Jesus. I hope that someday I will see him in heaven as I have heard that sometimes folks in a coma hear you but just can't respond. If he is there, and there is a porch on his heavenly home, I hope he is sitting there rocking away. I am sure, then, his signature greeting will have changed to, "It's wonderful, Wayne." I'll say, "It sure is." Then he'll reply, "Nah, it's better than that!"

Chapter 32

Clark and Alan

I have an old black and white picture of the Lyman Mission Assembly of God church's All Girls Band. Kneeling in front is my mom as a teenager, holding a guitar. Our neighbor, Zeke Holden, is the director, and among my mother's friends and fellow band members is Freda Nesmith, holding a mandolin. Freda, I remember well, because later in life, her two sons, Clark and Alan, were two of my best friends.

Clark was a few years older than me and was one of my heroes. I used to watch in awe as we played baseball. He was so smooth at fielding, hitting, or throwing that it amazed me. He could throw strikes from the outfield to home plate! It seemed to me that all of that just came natural to him whereas I had to work at it.

Clark's younger brother, Alan, didn't excel in sports as much, but if there was an adventure of some sort on our radar, you could count on Alan being in on it. I believe Alan was in the group of intrepid explorers I describe in the chapter, "The Bees and Me."

Up River

Certain memories seem to stand out in my mind when I think of Clark and Alan. One was the annual Lyman clean-up day each spring when folks would put piles of trash out on the streets and several crews of us young guys would come by, load it up, and haul it to the dump. Clark was old enough to drive so he drove the town's old retired and stripped-down firetruck and Alan and I were his crew. About ten on that Saturday morning we were working Reece Avenue where Clark and Alan lived, so when we got to their house, Clark stopped and yelled to us that he knew there was a box of powdered donuts inside. The three of us barged through the front door in a hurry. Oops! We barged in all right and scared the daylights out of their older sister who was not expecting visitors. She let out a blood curdling scream which sent us into an immediate about-face and back out the door. No donuts for us. We'd have to wait until noon to meet up with all the other crews at the city park for a big weenie roast. It seemed to me that almost the whole town showed up for that event which is one of the best memories I have of growing up in small town USA in the fifties and sixties.

Then, as it happens now and then, our tight gang of three got broken up when about 1960, the Nesmiths moved to Ballard, Washington, (a Seattle neighborhood) where Freda had gotten a good job. I missed those guys, but that enabled me to have the chance to go visit them several summers in a row. Their house was fairly close to the zoo and within walking distance of Green Lake, a local swimming hole. I don't remember going to the zoo, but I do remember that one warm night we snuck our way into the closed swimming area for a midnight swim.

I wasn't that good a swimmer, but not wanting to hear the dreaded catcall, "chicken!" I ventured out on the diving board, and dove into the dark water. I immediately sensed something was amiss, and what was amiss was my swimming trunks from my skinny 13-year old bean pole body. The impact of the water had stripped them off slick as a whistle. Adding to my sense of panic was that we had no towels and all we'd worn on that hot August night was our swim trunks and tennis shoes. A walk through that big city neighborhood wearing nothing but tennis shoes was NOT my idea of adventure.

So, all three of us were diving down again and again in that dark water until, finally, one of them snagged my floating trunks. As I recall, that evolved into a game of keep-away with Clark and Alan prolonging my desperation by tossing them back and forth just out of my reach. Finally, they relented, and we trudged back to their house.

Adulthood found me pastoring churches (mostly in Alaska),Clark working for a phone company, and Alan traveling all over the country setting up (and then dismantling) a traveling carnival. One day I got a call informing me that Alan had passed away and they asked if I could come down to our hometown of Lyman and officiate at his memorial service at the Lyman Baptist Church.

We gathered there where one side of the church sanctuary was filled with Alan's mother's old church friends and the other side was populated with a fair number of Alan's "carnie" friends and co-workers. After the formal part of the service, we had an "open mic" time when the group could share some of their memories and thoughts about Alan's life. The contrast was amusing as the church group shared their memories of Alan and the Nesmiths growing up in Sunday School and church in Lyman. The "carnie" side shared some humorous anecdotes of Alan's life "on the road" with them. Interestingly, they shared how Alan was a most generous person who, though he didn't have much, was always willing to help someone in need.

As Alan's family and ours gathered at my sister Glenice's

house, the day before the service, we all started sharing our own memories of Alan, but also how each of us remembered growing up in Lyman. It was a rich time as each person had a different perspective of memories of some of the colorful local people. The common thread, though, was that we all considered it a very special privilege to grow up in the little town of Lyman, population 400, give or take a few.

Chapter 33

Summer Romance

Perhaps if you looked up the word "brief" in a dictionary compiled by young teenagers, it might say: "The length of time it takes for a summertime romance to ignite, flourish, and then go kaput!" At least that is the way that phenomenon occurred in my young life.

The first melodrama was what my mom laughingly called a "strawberry patch romance" and boy, did I have one! Every summer, usually beginning as soon as school was out, the strawberries were ripening and the growers would hire us kids to help bring in the harvest. We'd ride to the berry patch with one of our moms or catch the "crew bus," arriving, lunch in hand, just as the sun was coming up.

The beginning of the berry-picking season also marked the arrival of a number of families that traveled around the area following whatever fruits or vegetables were in season to be harvested. Most were Hispanic. While most of us local kids were just picking berries to buy school clothes for the next year or to pay for summer camp, these families worked very hard together to support the family.

One particular season, it took me about five minutes to notice one particular Hispanic girl who was about my age and was absolutely beautiful. When she looked at me during the first break of the morning, blinked those dark brown eyes, and flashed a big smile revealing pearly white teeth, I was totally smitten! Then, when she spoke to me my knees almost buckled. However, being as shy as I was, I think I croaked out something resembling "Hi" back, turned and fled back to my row of berries. The problem was, the girls on the crew could usually pick circles around us boys and try as I might, this puppy-love-sick nerd just couldn't keep up.

Every morning for the duration of that two week season, I didn't need any coaxing to get out of bed, gobble a bowl of Wheaties, grab my lunch, and run out to the end of our driveway to catch the crew bus to the berry patch to, hopefully, have the love of my life smile at me again. Then suddenly, the berries were gone, the season was over, and we all lined up at the owner's truck to collect our paychecks. My heart sank when someone told me that the Hispanic families had already been paid and moved on to their next harvesting job. As for me, I took my paycheck and my little broken heart home, dug a can of worms, hopped on my bike, and spent the rest of the week, before the raspberries were ripe, fishing in Jones Creek and Minkler Lake while hoping against hope that her family might show up at the raspberry patch. It never happened. Gloom and despair descended on my life until Little League baseball started up for the summer.

Fast forward a few years where, by then, I had learned to operate tractors and other farm equipment. A warm sunny spring day found me driving a tractor with a silage chopper attached. Around and around a large field of clover I went as the chopper blew the cut grass out a chute and into the trucks that followed close by. Once they were full, they would head to the farm where the grass was forked into another blower and up to the top of a large domed silo.

It was a great job and I was now making the high pay of $2.50 an hour. I was in "high clover" as they say. It got really interesting when one day I noticed that there was a blonde girl leaning on a fence post near one of the farmhouses. Having gotten somewhat over the painfully shy stage, while full trucks were headed to the silo, I raised the chopper and wheeled the tractor over by the fence. Just being neighborly, you know! When I got close enough to see, I noticed that she was really a cutie. She was wearing that lime green eye shadow that was in vogue those days and bingo, there I was, smitten again. I didn't hesitate to agree to let her ride along with me on the tractor for a while. She acted all impressed at my skill at doing my job, so I asked if she wanted half of my peanut butter and jam sandwich for lunch while sitting in the shade of a tree, with our feet dangling off a log and into the cool water of nearby Jones Creek. I was convinced that, indeed, fate had brought us together, and I recall that we even smooched a couple of times before I had to get back to work. This was looking good!

That Saturday, she agreed to go to the rodeo with me, which was the beginning of the end. Her parting words were that she needed to go home the next day to the big city of Seattle. She promised to write to me every day. Then she added that the reason she was on her grandparents' farm was because she had been directed to rest and take it easy as she recovered from mono (mononucleosis). MONO!! I'd heard that you get that from kissing! Holy cow! I went to bed that night convinced that I would probably die from kissing! Sure enough, that night I woke up in a sweat, sicker than a dog! Well, it wasn't mono but I had eaten a greasy hamburger at the rodeo and had food poisoning! Of course, I never heard from her again. Now I was 0-2 in the summer romance department!

As I mentioned in another chapter, math was never my forte and that was especially evident in junior high when algebra was a required class. Thankfully, there was a really cute (and smart) gal sitting next to me who was good at math and was willing to help me. Somehow, I passed the class.

The next fall, there was a Girl Scout sponsored hayride and the girls were allowed to ask a boy if they wanted. My cute algebra tutor invited me, and though I was still very shy, I accepted. On that Saturday night, one of the scout mothers offered to pick me up along with her daughter and a couple other girls.

The night was ideal for a hayride with clear skies and a full harvest moon. We rode around a big pasture in a tractor-pulled hay wagon singing goofy songs before we wound up back at a big bonfire where we roasted weenies and marshmallows. Then, I had to say goodbye to my "date" and we piled back into the car for the ride back up the valley and home. It was a pretty special night all in all.

It had been pretty chilly so the driver cranked the car heater up full blast to warm us all up. However, with the heat pouring out, we all suddenly began to smell a really foul odor that was, without a doubt, akin to that which comes out of the north end of a southbound dog. The stench got worse as everyone in the car began accusing each other as the culprit that had "stepped in it." In the darkness of the car, it was anyone's guess.

I was the first person to be let out of the car at the end of our driveway. About halfway out the driveway, I wondered who was following me as that awful smell was still present. I stopped under the street lamp and checked my shoes. To my horror, I discovered IT WAS ME!! Yuck! I walked the rest of the way in the grass shuffling my feet trying to get that stinky mess off my shoe. I left the shoes in the woodshed and went in the house, grateful that the family was asleep so nobody asked me why I wasn't wearing my shoes.

Up to my room I went, humiliated to the core, knowing that once I'd left the car, the others would all know that I was the guilty one, and by Monday morning, the whole school would know what had happened, including my "date," who would probably never want to invite me anywhere, ever!

There are some embarrassing moments that happen to most of us as we journey through life, especially through adolescence, and often they cause us to make some powerful inner vows. I made one. No more dates for me, forever. I was now 0-3 in the romance department, and like baseball, three strikes and you're out.

Well, that lasted until the next spring when I started high school and managed to make the varsity baseball team. There was this gorgeous brunette with a cool flip hairdo and a great smile who started to attend the games. When she gave me THAT smile…oh no, there I was, smitten once more. Dare I try again?

Chapter 34

Music and Me

I have a picture of my mom and me sitting on the piano bench in our house in Lyman; and that is probably where my love of music started. My mom taught herself how to play the piano and could read and play sheet music, as well as play "by ear." She would play from old (very old) gospel songbooks. Sometimes my sisters would join in, and we'd sing and harmonize for an hour or two with our dad as the audience. He'd share his appreciation of our efforts in spite of the regular sour notes.

Mom signed me up for piano lessons when I was 6 or 7, long before I had the motivation to practice for the old gal that came to the house to teach my lesson. She was a nice lady, but I was not a willing pupil. I do remember one song about week two of my lessons; it was "Here We Go a-Fishing." And the following week, that is what I opted to do before she arrived. I think the next week I hid out in the corn patch and did not respond when my mom called and whistled for me. My mom and the teacher agreed that I was not "ready" for piano lessons. Like lots of washed out piano students, I sincerely regret not sticking with it.

Fifth grade music class was one of my favorites, as it was much more fun than math or spelling. We'd sit in rows with old American folk song books and sing songs like "The Ballad of Davy Crockett," "Blow the Man Down," and "Ivan Skavinsky Skavar." I did not overly enjoy the mandatory lessons in playing those song flutes, a skill I never came close to mastering.

Then also in fifth grade the music teacher encouraged us to pick an instrument we might like to play and I picked the trumpet. First, I used a loaner from the school until I got one of my very own, a cheap model from the music store in Sedro Woolley. I stuck with it and eventually got a fancier model which I played in the band and orchestra all through school.

During my early years as an aspiring trumpeter, about all I could produce was an obnoxious "blatt" and I remember my mom ordering me to take that thing out to the barn to practice. I complied with her order but the cows, chickens, and pigs all ducked for cover.

In high school, I was the student director of the "Pep Band" which played the "Star-Spangled Banner" and a number of "fight songs" for the home basketball games. That was fun since quality music wasn't really the goal, but LOUD music was!

As a trumpet player, probably my greatest honor was to be asked by the veterans in our town on Memorial Day to be the one to stand across the street from the cemetery behind a massive cedar tree to play "Taps" in honor of those who had served and given their lives for our country. I was really nervous, because one of the veterans standing at attention after the 21-gun salute, was my dad.

After high school, I turned my love of music to singing. My freshman year in college I was able to be a part of a gospel quartet called the Kinsmen. That summer we were selected as one of several groups to travel for three months to numerous churches and Bible camps doing concerts and presenting what the college had to offer interested prospective students.

That's me standing in the middle, leaning on the bass singer's shoulder.

In later life, the high point of my musical endeavors was when I became a worship leader at a church in Anchorage, Alaska, during the 70's. Being surrounded by a group of incredibly talented musicians and singers, and a large enthusiastic congregation, made this a wonderful experience. Probably the biggest blessing that I experienced during those years was when the sister of a young disabled boy shared with me that just prior to his passing away, his family had asked him when in his life that he felt the closest to God. He answered that it was when he was in church and Pastor Wayne was leading worship. That still brings tears to my eyes.

Chapter 35

Flag Football

Back in the fifties, we took our sports seriously at the Lyman Grade School. For the small size of the school, we had pretty good football, basketball, and track teams. Most of our success was thanks to Tony Fore (in my grade) who was arguably one of the best all-around athletes in the area. He had real muscles and could run really fast, even in 5th and 6th grades. In basketball, it didn't hurt either that we had Ivan Bacus, who was about six feet tall and towered over the other boys. I remember that we played against schools in Sedro Woolley, Clear Lake, and Hamilton.

Mr. Rowe, the 5th and 6th grade teacher, school principal, and coach worked us hard during recess learning to catch football passes or baseball fly balls. He could hit us fly balls that seemed a mile high. On rainy days, he'd have us run pass patterns in the gym and pay us a penny for each pass we caught out of his little rubber coin holder that would open up as he squeezed it. I remember the football sidelines being lined with parents and, of course, really cute cheerleaders belting out "Two bits, four bits, six bits, a dollar, all for Lyman, stand up and holler."

At that level, we played flag football through 8th grade. I stuck with it up into 8th grade in Junior High in Sedro Woolley. They played tackle football after that. However somewhere about mid -season in 8th grade I made a discovery. I was allergic to pain! I played defensive end on the kick-offs. That position required that NO MATTER WHAT I was never supposed to let the guy with the ball get past me on that side of the field. I did OK most of the time. However, one day, on a kickoff, the guy running with the ball was clear over on the other side of the field and I was "staying in my lane" like I was supposed to do while the action was elsewhere. Not paying much attention, I did not see a big guy coming to block me when, WHAM, he hit me so hard it knocked me out cold. The next thing I remember was waking up on the sidelines after the manager put some smelling salts under my nose. When my eyes started to focus, I saw several of the cheerleaders come over to me to see if I was dead or alive. I had a bad headache and decided then and there that I'd go out for baseball, band, and maybe girls.

Chapter 36

Grand Theft Cherries

Whoever said that "stolen strawberries always taste sweeter," could have been from Lyman. While I am certainly not advocating breaking the 7th Commandment about stealing, I do remember fudging on that one during my formative years a couple of times. I also learned that axiom about sweet fruit also applied to cherries as well.

One lazy summer day my cousin and I got a hankerin' for some of those pink and yellow Royal Ann cherries that were ripe and hanging thick on an old cherry tree, in a farmer's pasture next to the grade school playground. No one ever seemed to pick those cherries except, perhaps, the robins, crows, and pigeons, so we figured it was no big deal.

We managed to climb up near the top of the tree and spent several hours eating those delicious cherries and spitting the pits at each other. It was really an idyllic way for a couple of young guys to while away a summer afternoon. That was until our reverie was interrupted by that old farmer who came out on the edge of the field and yelled at us "hoodlums" to get out of his cherry tree. Believe me, we came down out of that tree a lot faster than we went up it. Once we hit the ground, we crawled through the high grass toward a barbed-wire fence which we snuck under and made our escape into the cemetery.

As we were walking down the little dirt road, leading out of the cemetery and toward home, the logical results of a belly full of cherries hit my cousin with an urgent need to find a place to relieve the pressure. Into the high grass he ran where he dropped his britches just in time to download things. Suddenly he let out a loud yelp and came bursting out of the grass, hopping up and down while trying to button up his jeans. It turns out that he had squatted down into a very virulent patch of stinging nettles that made his posterior feel like it was on fire!

He easily outran me to his house where his mom doctored him up with some Calamine lotion, along with a well-timed lecture on how our sins would "find us out." Along with that was a strong exhortation that next time it would be best to ask permission from that farmer (actually a nice man) before trespassing and snitching any more of his cherries.

Chapter 37

Cougar!

At the east end of the Lyman swamp was an old barbed wire fence that was mostly submerged in the dark water. Up against the fence, years ago, someone had built a makeshift bridge using fence posts, some pallets, and some planks from a nearby collapsing barn. The water there was 4 or 5 feet deep, but if you were careful, you could pick your way across that treacherous span to reach the other side where there was an abandoned railroad grade along the base of Prevedel Hill, and where there was a long stretch of flourishing and very sweet blackberries.

One nice autumn day, after a game of football, five or six of us decided to cross the "bridge" and eat our fill of those juicy berries. It was tricky going, but we made it across and were walking west into the glare of the setting sun, laughing and having fun, when one of the guys exclaimed that there was a big dog walking toward us. That, in itself, was no big deal, until we noticed that the "dog" had a mighty long tail as he sashayed from side to side of the path.

Almost in unison, we all recognized this wasn't a dog at all, but instead, a big cougar. No doubt he was preoccupied in trying to find a rabbit or pheasant for dinner, but to us, we were convinced that he was stalking us. No one needed to shout, "Run!" as we were already making tracks as fast as we could go toward that bridge not even daring to look back to see if that predator was on our heels.

Not being very fleet afoot, even with an adrenaline boost, I was the last of the guys to reach the bridge. Not pausing a second to map a careful course to avoid a dip into the swamp water, I skipped and jumped from plank to plank and, in a few places, felt I was imitating the Apostle Peter by walking on the water! Once we were across the bridge and up the slope on the other side, we all plopped down on the grass to catch our breath. We had escaped the clutches and fangs of that monster killer cougar.

One of the guys ran home and told his dad what had happened. His dad hightailed it down to the tavern, where he told the story to one of the regular patrons who happened to have a pack of hunting dogs. Later that night, he and some of his hunting pals and dogs got on the trail of the cougar and shot it. The word spread around Lyman, and the cougar could be seen in the back of a pickup at the tavern. This was sad, of course, for the cougar who was just minding his own business, but for us "brave" swamp pirates, we were all local heroes for a day or two for our part in bringing that marauding, vicious cat to justice. However, we all knew that we were not the brave boys they thought we were, we had just run for our lives and almost walked on the black waters of the old Lyman Swamp.

Chapter 38

Dad's Sidekick

I suppose when you are a kid, one of life's grand adventures was when you would get to tag along with Dad to his work. That was certainly the case for me.

My dad worked for 30 years as an occupational therapist at the large mental hospital in Sedro Woolley. He was also an LPN and an x-ray technician. I remember walking down those long halls with high ceilings and hard tile floors, hearing the echo with every step. It was kind of a spooky place to me, but I was with Dad, so it was OK.

His was a fairly small office with two desks, one for him and one for a co-worker. Usually, when I was able to tag along with him, the extra desk was unoccupied and I was able to spend hours pecking away at an old manual typewriter while Dad worked on his files. Usually we ate our sandwiches for lunch, but occasionally we would walk over to the "Canteen" snack bar for a hamburger and a coke.

Sometimes, I would get to go with him to the x-ray lab and go into the dark room where the x-rays were developed. That was a fascinating process to see how they could actually take pictures of someone's bones right through their skin.

During my teenage years, most of our working together occurred on our small farm. My dad was also in charge of the public works department for the town so on many Saturdays we would fix leaks in the water system, do maintenance on the dump, cemetery, or city park. On Sunday afternoons we would hike several miles up in the hills to the small dam to clean the screens that filtered the water of Jones Creek before the water started its gravity flow journey to the homes in town.

I remember Dad got paid $1.50 an hour for his work and I got paid $1.00 an hour for mine. That was big bucks for a kid back then.

In retrospect, I don't think I always had a true understanding or appreciation of what it meant to work with my dad. Often, I'd rather have been playing ball or fishing. But, when my dad came home from World War II and began to build a life for our family, he sometimes worked two or three jobs and didn't have much time for recreation. By having me work with him, he'd found a way to spend time with his son and I got to know my dad.

Chapter 39

Unsweet Revenge

High school romance is indeed a tumultuous passage in life to be sure. Most last a few days, weeks, or even months, but occasionally it would appear that a young love would be the real deal and high school sweethearts would marry, have a family, and live happily ever after. My junior year I was totally smitten by the love bug for a really sweet girl. We were both dedicated Christian students, belonged to several after school clubs, and even had a few classes that we shared.

In our family, our dad was famous for playing little practical jokes and teasing in a good-natured way. So, it was pretty much in my DNA to tease and joke around with my girlfriend. One class that we shared was sociology, and my desk was right behind hers. Sometimes we would pass notes back and forth and, fortunately, never got caught doing that forbidden deed.

Well, one day as the teacher was droning on and on, my "sweet" friend was sharing a bag of M&Ms with me by secretly handing a few at a time back to me, and I'd discretely slip them into my mouth. I'd usually just suck on them until the candy coating would dissolve and the tasty chocolate insides were exposed. In one handful of M&Ms she had snuck in something about the same size and color as an M&M, and into my mouth it went. After about 30-seconds, I bit down on the goodies and "crunch," I had bitten down on a vitamin pill! Have you ever tasted one of those things without the coating? They are more bitter than your average bitter and simply taste gnarly! I was gagging and coughing and dying for a drink of water to get that nasty taste out of my mouth while it was all my "sweetie" could do to muffle her laughter. When the bell rang to dismiss the class, I made a beeline to the nearest water fountain. Indeed, the lesson is true, you reap what you sow! However, that DNA link I inherited from my dad was never dormant for long as my kids will attest.

Probably one of my all-time best capers was when the girls were in their early teens. One day, I got one of those finger-sized "Tootsie Rolls", chewed it up a little until I could form it into what, for all the world, looked similar to what would come out of the north end of a south-bound dog. I then strategically placed it on one of the girl's bedspreads where the dog often took naps. Waiting nearby, I heard my daughter scream, "Daaaad! That dog pooped on my bed!" Rushing to the rescue, I looked down on the offending item and casually remarked, "Well, I do believe she did." Then, I reached down, picked it up, and popped it into my mouth and began chewing. I still laugh at how she screamed, "Oh gross" and made a dash for the hallway gagging and yelling not nice words to me. I think she has forgiven me but if that DNA thing gets passed on from generation to generation, I suspect that someday it will be payback time.

Chapter 40

Archie and On-ey

Far and away, my favorite fishing partner was my dad. Whether it was fishing on the Skagit River for steelhead, or trout fishing in a lake or one of the local small streams, my dad seemed to know where to go, how to catch fish, and (most of the time) was a patient teacher.

However, my dad had a regular job year-round as an occupational therapist at Northern State Hospital which left me without a fishing partner in the summer. In later years I'd learned enough for my parents to trust me to fish on the river alone, but before that, I was allowed to go next door to see if Archie Angel and his pal, On-ey (pronounced Awney) Jackson (both retired) were going over to "the slough" (a slow moving backwater spot on the river) trout fishing and to ask if they'd mind if I tagged along. More often than not, they were going and let me come along.

I remember clearly that they used to take their worms in Prince Albert tobacco cans that would fit in the pouch of their old bib overalls. I carried mine in a Folger's coffee can. It was about a half mile walk up the road, across the railroad tracks by the cemetery, and down an old rutted, muddy road that ran parallel to the tracks until it came to their "un-secret" fishing spot. The older gentlemen took their time moseying over there so I had to force myself to walk at their pace.

There was just enough room for the three of us to sit on the bank or a rock, cast our lines out, prop our poles up on forked alder sticks in the sand, and wait for a bite. Getting bites usually didn't take too long, but often you would reel in a small but extremely ugly bullhead or a lethargic old sucker. However, there were also plenty of trout which were the desired prize.

Bringing home a stringer of 6-8" trout was always a matter of pride for me. Next would come a trip out to the covered patio with a sink and running water to clean the catch. The family rule was, "You catch 'em, you clean 'em." That night, Mom would dip them in milk, roll them in corn meal, and fry them in bacon grease. It was a meal fit for a king and tasty indeed. I'd swell with pride that I'd "brought home the bacon," so to speak. Oh, I should add, Mom always fried the smaller fish with their tails attached...a delicacy as they were sort of like homemade potato chips. Finger lickin' good!

Chapter 41

Sunday School and Church Camp

I have a little round pin with a tiny removable insert that means that I had near perfect attendance in Sunday School at the Lyman Mission Church (Assembly of God) for eleven consecutive years. Once a year I got to walk to the front of the congregation and be awarded a new insert with one more year added. I was really proud of that pin.

The Mission wasn't a large church, maybe a hundred people, but it was a big part of our lives. My mom was the Sunday School superintendent, and along with other duties, she always made sure us kids got our Saturday night bath, studied our Sunday School lesson, and wore our Sunday-best clothes the next day.

The most memorable Sunday School teacher I can remember was Lou Shellman, who made those old Bible stories come alive for us kids. She was really good and knew how to keep our attention; no small feat with a small room filled with squirmy adolescent kids.

After all those years, I had memorized all the books of the Bible in proper order, and had most all of the Bible stories down pretty well, and could usually stand and deliver the weekly memory verse on cue. I still, years later, enjoy reading of the exploits of David with Goliath and Daniel in the lion's den.

There were usually enough workers and young people to put on the annual Christmas and Easter plays, which drew a large crowd of folks in the community who did not normally attend that church. The Christmas event usually featured one of the older men dressed up like Santa Claus who would pass out bags of candy to everyone present. During one of the Christmas plays, (about a man coming home for the holidays) one of the actors really botched his lines and the whole cast and those present burst into laughter and the play came to a standstill. Once the folks stopped laughing and the play was about to continue, sure enough, someone would start laughing again and everyone joined in laughing until the tears were flowing.

Other yearly highlights were summer Vacation Bible School and the all-church picnic. VBS was a fun time when we'd learn songs with lots of motions, learn Bible verses, and do craft projects. For several years the special speaker was also a chalk artist who would do a picture, using special chalk which, when the lights were turned off and a "black light" was turned on, the whole thing would glow in the dark, amidst genuine "oohs" and "aahs" from all the kids and adults. I remember carving a cross from a bar of Ivory soap (bring your own soap) and gluing the words of John 3:16 on a paper plate using uncooked alphabet soup letters. Two years in a row I won the first prize for bringing the most people to the evening VBS session. The first year the prize was a chintzy baseball mitt, but the next year it was a five-foot tall candy bar in the shape of a cross. It had a chicken wire frame inside and had a bunch of candy bars attached and covered with aluminum foil. I had to share the loot with all 54 people whom I had invited!

The biggest event of the year by far was the Sunday School or all-church picnic. It was often held at Larabee State Park, which featured a big ball field, covered tables—in case of rain, and a salt water beach where we could swim or search for crabs. The food was pot luck, but let me tell you, those mostly southern-raised ladies could really make great fried chicken and potato salad. The church provided the ice cream and watermelon. By the end of the day, we kids were pretty tuckered out, the ladies were tired of sitting in the shade swapping stories, and the men had crowned the horseshoe tossing champion for yet another year.

The most lasting memory I have of that little church was when I was five years-old, I realized I needed to ask Jesus personally to come into my heart and I went forward to the altar at the end of a service and did just that. To this day, I am grateful for all the people who worked and kept that little church alive, and a blessing, for many years.

There was an old song that we used to sing, and at the time I didn't care much for, but now it has special meaning. The song was "Precious Memories." I think all that remains of that church building is a cement slab but every time I visit Lyman, I almost think I can hear that old song reverberating in my soul.